THE POWER OF DIGITAL IDENTITY

Rakesh Soni

THE
POWER OF
DIGITAL
IDENTITY

Winning Customer Trust and
Transforming Experience

COPYRIGHT © 2025 RAKESH SONI
All rights reserved.

THE POWER OF DIGITAL IDENTITY
Winning Customer Trust and Transforming Experience

FIRST EDITION

ISBN 978-1-5445-4626-1 *Hardcover*
      978-1-5445-4625-4 *Paperback*
      978-1-5445-4624-7 *Ebook*

To my mom and dad,
who always believed in me
and unconditionally supported my life decisions.

CONTENTS

A NOTE ON TERMINOLOGY 9
INTRODUCTION 11

PART ONE: DIGITAL IDENTITY
1. THE EVOLUTION OF IDENTITY 25
2. THE ECONOMIC IMPACT OF DIGITAL IDENTITY 31
3. ENTERPRISE IAM VS. CUSTOMER IAM 37

PART TWO: THE CURRENT STATE AND OPPORTUNITY OF CONSUMER IDENTITY
4. CONSUMER TRENDS AND KEY ISSUES 47
5. REALIZING THERE'S A PROBLEM 63
6. CONNECTING THE DOTS 73
7. UNDERSTANDING THE IMPACT 79

PART THREE: STRATEGY AND DEVELOPMENT OF YOUR CIAM PROGRAM
8. STRATEGIZING A CIAM SOLUTION AND IDENTIFYING THE PIECES 89
9. CIAM REFERENCE ARCHITECTURE 101
10. CONSUMER IDENTITY EXPERIENCE: DESIGN AND DEVELOPMENT 117
11. CIAM SECURITY AND PRIVACY: DESIGN AND DEVELOPMENT 127
12. FLOW OF DIGITAL ID IN YOUR ECOSYSTEM 137
13. CIAM ESSENTIAL CAPABILITIES 147
14. CIAM SELECTION AND DESIGN FRAMEWORK 163
15. CIAM BEST PRACTICES 173

PART FOUR: CIAM
16. SEEING THE BENEFITS 185
17. DEFINING YOUR OWN ROI 195
18. BUILDING VS. BUYING 199
19. LEARNING FROM OTHERS 205

PART FIVE: THE FUTURE
20. BEING READY FOR THE FUTURE 211
21. KEEPING UP WITH INNOVATION 229

CONCLUSION 231
ACKNOWLEDGMENTS 233
ABOUT THE AUTHOR 235

A NOTE ON TERMINOLOGY

When we talk about **customers**, we're referring to *businesses*, not individual consumers. "Customers," in our parlance, are the businesses that buy CIAM software. When we talk about the general public, we call them **users, end-users**, or **consumers**.

There are two huge exceptions to this rule:

1. When we talk about CIAM, which literally stands for Customer Identity and Access Management, "customer" means—in that context—the individual consumer who interacts with brands and their websites.
2. The subtitle of this book is "winning *customer* trust and transforming experience." We deliberately went against our own rule there so as not to confuse casual book-buyers.

INTRODUCTION

Trust Is Everything

According to Forrester Research, the average loss in revenue to the company when someone loses or forgets their password and requires a reset is a staggering $70 per user.[1] How is that possible?

Turns out that, for most people, **if they run into problems when trying to reset their password, they get frustrated and leave altogether.**

There are many reasons that a simple password reset can fail. Sometimes, you just get tired of trying different variations and having the website tell you that your entry is unacceptable (too short, used before, etc.). Or if you succeed in getting past that threshold, sometimes the email response with the temporary password gets lost in your spam filter, and you give up.

Occasionally, it's the system itself that doesn't work. Maybe the page doesn't load, and the request is never submitted.

---

[1] Merritt Maxim and Andras Cser, "Best Practices: Selecting, Deploying, and Managing Enterprise Password Managers," Forrester, January 8, 2018, https://www.forrester.com/report/best-practices-selecting-deploying-and-managing-enterprise-password-managers/RES139333.

Point is, when password resets get tricky, users get grumpy and simply go away. In the case of United, when they broke down the sum of all their lost revenue from this problem, it was the equivalent of $15 per person!

We bring this up because it shows just how important **consumer experience** is in today's world. Password resets are all about experience: When someone struggles, they have a *bad* experience—and that's why they leave.

A bad user experience is often remembered long after the initial event. It doesn't have to be something as dramatic as a security breach or as constant as a bad attitude—it could be an everyday occurrence and still leave a very bad impression.

Experience, however, is only one of the pillars that support the problems we address in this book. The bigger story here is **digital identity** and how to harness its power to provide a secure and privacy compliant experience and win customer trust.

When someone signs up for, say, an online newspaper, they're giving the publication sensitive details about their identity. Of course, it's important for the company to protect that user account. After all, the subscriber is taking a huge leap of faith in trusting that their information is secure.

Along the same lines, it's essential that the newspaper be trusted to act in compliance with the law and follow privacy regulations around their users' data.

The good news: If the newspaper is on top of all this and knows how to successfully manage customer identity, it will create trust and make it more likely that the user will have a good experience. They may even feel *delighted* by the relationship.

But this can only happen if proper attention is paid to **security, privacy,** and **experience**.

It is needed now more than ever.

HOW DID WE GET HERE?

Over the last ten years, we saw two major consumer trends in the arena of digital identity.

First, with the arrival of high-speed internet and, particularly, mobile phones, everything became accessible digitally. In the old days, we would drive around late at night looking for a place to eat that was still open. Now, of course, we just consult our reliable food delivery app. The way people think about buying from eating establishments has changed completely.

Similarly, we went from trying to hail a yellow cab to just opening an app and booking from a ride-sharing service.

Because of this monumental shift, consumers began to *expect* amazing experiences. No longer were they satisfied with whatever was available. They wanted what they wanted when they wanted: *the right information at the right time and in the right way*. It didn't matter who you were (a bank, a media company, an e-commerce outlet)—if you couldn't give them that amazing experience, they were gone. Out.

Then came trend number two. With all these new services online—and with billions of people on billions of phones browsing billions of websites—a huge amount of data was being created, data that companies could exploit for profit.

Eventually, this led to a wave of public outcry, which forced governments around the world to start enacting privacy regulations, such as the European Union's (EU) General Data Protection Regulation (GDPR) legislation and the California Consumer Privacy Act (CCPA).

Meanwhile, as hackers and cybercriminals saw that they could make money by stealing data, they became more active. This led to an increase in data breaches around the world (a problem that is only getting worse).

It was in this environment—where trust in businesses was

plummeting and expectations were continually rising—that consumers began favoring more trustworthy, experience-focused companies.

It all led to a fundamental shift in consumer behavior over the past decade.

WHAT DOES THIS MEAN FOR YOU?

On the regulation front, there are only going to be *more* privacy laws in the future, and they will become ever more complex. It shouldn't be a surprise that the world has come a long way since the concept of data privacy was first introduced. According to the United Nations, a staggering 128 out of 194 countries have legislation requiring how their citizens' data should be protected.[2]

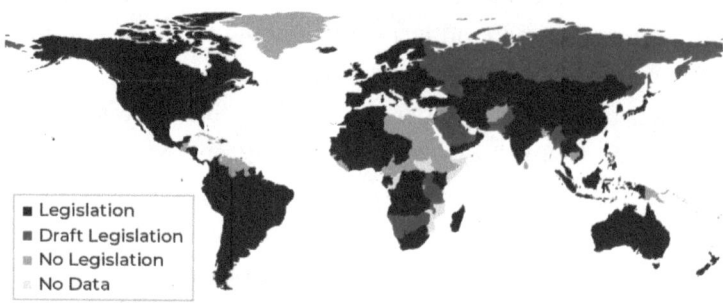

Privacy law, which has traditionally been a legal problem, is now also a technology problem. If users want—and are allowed by law—to see their information, then engineers need to build the functionality for that. And when companies are forced to

---

2   UN Trade and Development, "Data Protection and Privacy Legislation Worldwide," accessed May 9, 2023, https://unctad.org/page/data-protection-and-privacy-legislation-worldwide.

seek consent before interacting with their customers digitally, compliance can become a technological nightmare.

As for security, the kinds of breaches we've seen over the past five to seven years are only becoming more frequent. Not only do they cause a great deal of anguish to consumers, but they tarnish a company's reputation and can often bring it down—to the tune of hundreds of millions of dollars in government fines.

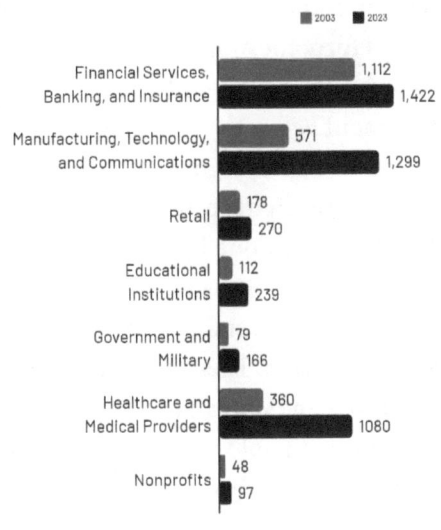

Source: Privacy Rights Clearinghouse, 2023

It's true that the Googles of the world are getting fined for privacy breaches. But it can happen to anyone. Creating and maintaining a safe online environment for consumers is a huge liability, and we know that **once your brand is damaged, it's five to ten times harder to acquire new customers and earn back that lost revenue.**

How do you protect yourself in this volatile environment?

Here's how: Use the power of digital identity to *meet the growing expectation around user experience and win back consumers' trust.*

CIAM (Customer Identity and Access Management) makes it possible.

WHAT IS CIAM?

When you look at any digital interaction, it's the same basic sequence. A visitor comes to a website or app and signs up. Then, when they return, they log back in.

There are a few different stages to the interaction, though: first, the brief moment *before* they log in, then the *active access* period, which lasts until they sign out. This is the typical journey of any user with any digital property, whether a website or mobile app. All of us have done it—dozens or even hundreds of times.

But when you look a little closer at the journey, you see that it's made up of two elements. There is the *human* side, the experience of going through the stages, and the *information* side, the packet of personal identifiable information (PII) (first name, last name, birthday, etc.) attached to you and your account that flows with you through your entire digital journey.

On the human side of the equation, whenever a visitor comes in, they are greeted with a set of products or product lines, as well as many other ingredients designed to create an experience.

> How do you deliver an experience that fulfills the human element of the user's digital journey?

Then, on the information side, the question is this: What do you do to protect the information from both a security and privacy perspective?

And, crucially, how do you combine the two? **How do you secure their data and identity as the users go through the different stages of the experience?**

These are the questions that every company needs to ask themselves.

Thankfully, there are answers out there, and they all run through modern technology. Companies can either develop solutions in-house or they can partner with outside experts. But if they want to win their users' trust and protect users' identity and data throughout the consumer journey, they have to do *something*.

If you don't act on these issues, you'll end up in the cold.

Unfortunately, too many businesses remain largely blind to industry trends and what's happening in digital transformation. They don't know how the security space is evolving or what's new in the privacy space. They don't fully understand how the digital/mobile market has created an *experience quotient*.

And they certainly don't understand CIAM. They are still confused between customer identity and *internal* identity management, which, granted, has a very similar name (IAM, which stands for Identity Access and Management).

IAM has been around for much longer than CIAM. In fact, the tech company IBM (sorry for all the similar abbreviations!) used an IAM solution with its employees over twenty-five years ago. But it's only been in the last eight to ten years that CIAM has emerged on the scene, with companies using software solutions from third-party vendors to manage consumer identity.

> IAM and CIAM are not *at all* the same thing!

WHAT CIAM CAN DO FOR YOU

If you're like a lot of people we talk to (CIOs, CTOs, CDOs, CISCOs, etc.), your brand's digital identity problem boils down to this: **you're managing identity—security, experience, and privacy—***in literally dozens of different applications.*

What do we mean by this?

Especially at large Fortune 5000 companies, you likely have multiple user touchpoints. The user goes to your website, your mobile app, your sister brand, your international website, your tech support line...the list goes on and on, and each of these login systems has its own way of identifying the person.

What ends up happening is that, through these many different interactions, the user inevitably creates multiple identities with the same company.

The problem is that each of these systems has its own way of identifying the user, its own login mechanism. When someone goes to a physical store, they are identified using their credit card information. Then, when they go to the same store online, they are asked for their email address and password. And when they go to the mobile app, they have to create a username and password.

 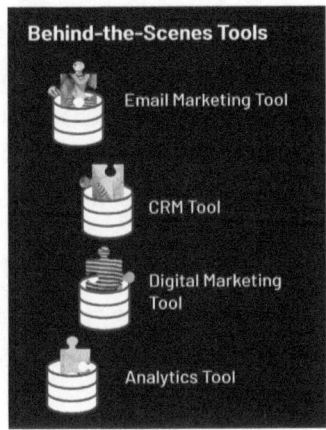

Clearly, this state of affairs is far from optimal. It creates a **broken experience for the user** because they need to identify themselves again and again at every touchpoint.

Meanwhile, on the company's side, they end up having to keep all these balls in the air at the same time—managing security, experience, and privacy at all these different places in what are called **identity silos**. Because each of the different teams are trying to manage identity in their own way, it becomes impossible for the company's global security department to enforce compliance.

Furthermore, the company's engineers now have to manage these awkward, out-the-box solutions at twenty different places! Identity becomes not just a security, experience, and privacy problem, but an engineering problem too.

Sadly, that is how it is at most companies.

The beauty of CIAM solutions is that they break down these silos.

Using CIAM to tackle the problems around security, experience, and privacy—even engineering—one begins to see that the problems are in fact not distinct from one another but part of the same stew of identity issues. They are all linked.

In the following chapters, we will see how *CIAM works to solve the whole puzzle.*

Simply put, it is *the* mission-critical piece that you've been looking for.

Use the power of digital identity to win trust and transform user experience.

WHAT YOU WILL LEARN

You're reading this book because you're interested in building better identity solutions for your business. This book will help you get a solid grounding in CIAM fundamentals, broaden your understanding of the space, and learn how to apply CIAM strategies to solve a particular problem you have in your company.

In the following chapters, we walk you through the ins and outs of CIAM, what it is, why it matters, and how you should strategize it—so you can win trust and transform your users' experience.

Ultimately, **by delivering a secure and delightful experience, you'll see higher consumer satisfaction, higher revenue, and greater protection** from cyber threats, as well as be able to mitigate legal liabilities from privacy law violations.

Every reader's situation is different, but by learning about CIAM, you will correlate and apply it to your scenario, using these tools to augment your own business. The more you come to understand about digital identity through the course of this book, the more you will be able to identify the root of the problems within your own company.

You will learn how to use CIAM to effectively manage customer identity to grow your business.

Growth means more new users attracted to your business and fewer slipping out the side door.

This book *will* help you define and deploy your own customer identity strategy. By working to solve those challenges around identity, you will almost certainly see the impact on your business and bottom line.

It's important for us to clarify too that this *isn't* a technical book. You won't find in these pages any specific engineering how-tos or one-size-fits-all steps for implementing your unique identity solution. It's certainly not a book about any one specific software product.

Rather, what we are putting forth here is a general guide for helping readers define and deploy *their own customer identity strategy*—as well as an important overview of **what CIAM is, why it matters, and what the business benefits are.**

WHO WE ARE

Both of us are engineers. We may not have been the first to get into the CIAM game, but together we were pioneers in making this type of solution available in the market.

Over the past few years, we've worked with thousands of companies—including many Fortune 5000 organizations—to deploy these strategies on a large scale. In helping these leaders solve their identity problems, we gained tremendous knowledge and experience, and now we are sharing our learning with you.

For this book, we drew not only on our core competencies as engineers and the results of our past consulting practices, but also on the wealth of data security and identity protection research that we have done in developing our own CIAM product, LoginRadius, and building our company around it.

The two of us were drawn together because we shared an interest in working on a problem that would have widespread effects: digital identity.

The concept of digital identity has changed how we interact with one another, not just in terms of the way we relate but also in how we identify ourselves to others.

What we have learned over the years is that any issue with digital identity goes *deep*. It's not just about technology or security. It touches every facet of a business.

PART ONE

DIGITAL IDENTITY

A Fundamental Human Right

CHAPTER ONE

THE EVOLUTION OF IDENTITY

What is identity?

This book may be new, but the subject of identity and our struggles around it go back centuries.

For our earliest ancestors, identity meant somebody's *face*. People recognized faces, and that's how they identified one another.

Then *names* came into the mix. Humans began going by personalized monikers. But that created a new problem: How to identify individuals who shared the same name.

So we started adding onto the name: What *tribe* were we from, what was our *family* name?

And that was that—for many, many years.

But as populations grew and people started clustering in larger groups, in cities, **identity became more complicated.** Governments and ruling organizations began needing more sophisticated ways to keep track of their people.

Identity started incorporating *physical address*—and from

there, more differentiators ultimately emerged (birthday, title, profession). Drivers' licenses, passports, social security cards, and other such items were used to package and organize information and establish identity.

Of course, when computers came on the scene, identity was drastically transformed once again. "Usernames" and email addresses became the new unique identifiers.

Amazon, launched in 1995, was integral to the evolution of digital identity. But it wasn't until the early 2000s that people became truly comfortable sharing their personal credit card or bank information online.

Then, in the late 2000s, mobile technology changed the game yet again. The extraordinary **rise of the smartphone meant that identity shifted from emails and usernames to cell phone numbers.**

With the mass adoption of mobile—as well as widespread access to high-speed internet—people's *standards* also rose dramatically. As discussed in the Introduction, users began to expect a lot more in terms of customer experience and how services were delivered to them. Consumers sued companies that lagged in this regard.

Meanwhile, the need for security—and the threat of security breaches—reached new highs.

With the advent of social media, companies like Facebook weren't only keeping a profile of user information like name, gender, etc., they were building vast social profiles of what users liked, what their friends liked, and much more.

The stakes were higher than ever.

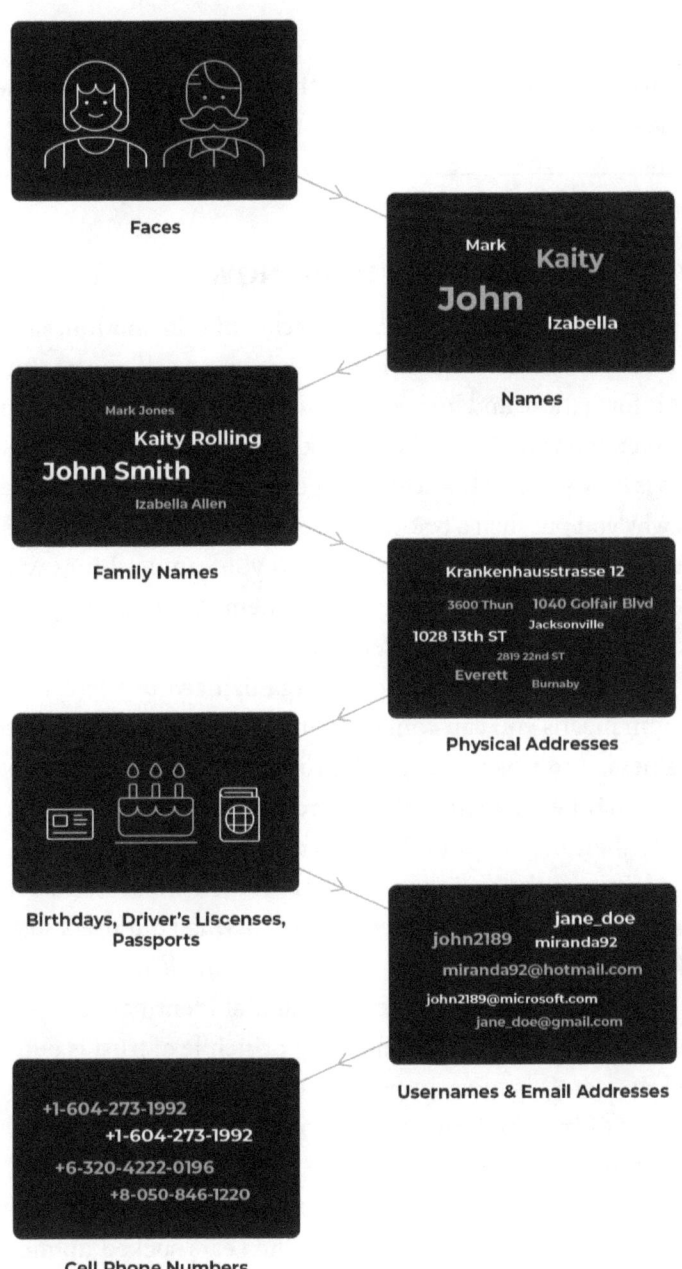

> Identity has long preoccupied the human mind, and the issues around it have been part of our lives for centuries.

WHAT DOES IDENTITY MEAN NOW

At the end of the day, identity is a **packet of information**, same as it's always been. What's changed is how we gather and store the information, and how we use this identity. Most important between then and now is how you keep it secure and organized. This is how you create a seamless, personalized user experience. It's why you put such a priority on securing and organizing your users' identities in the first place—so you can do things with them, serve them, and connect with them. All these things are made possible because of identity.

Think about it: Securing and organizing your users' information means you can contact them. If you're an e-commerce business, it means you can sell products. It's what allows you to attach other elements, like a purchase history or a shopping list, to their information. *It's how companies scale.*

Identity is the basis of our users' relationships with us. It's fundamental to their experience. And so, when our users share information with us, we protect it and secure it.

In other words, the benefits of digital identity come with great responsibility. The underlying principle of trust is perennial. In fact, it is more important than ever, given that these packets of information—which constitute identity in todays' digital world—have so many more layers and risks involved.

What used to be a basic customer profile with information like username and gender has over the years sucked up more and more data. Social media expanded the customer profile to incorporate *social* profiles (who are a user's friends, what do they like, what don't they like?).

As much as some things have stayed the same, identity has evolved. What was simply a packet of information to identify someone has become more **like a contract between two parties**. The user is willing to give their identifying information in exchange for the promise of a good, secure experience.

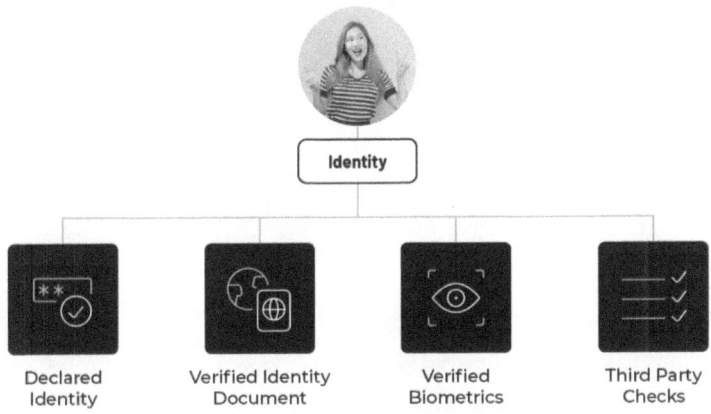

Identity is no longer simply defined by a single label. There are new security and privacy issues to consider, which add responsibilities for the entity in possession of that information.

Through the evolution of identity—from its offline version to digital—protecting the privacy of the customer has always been important, and it is going to remain so even when identity evolves into something else a hundred years from now.

Reinforcing this fundamental responsibility over identity is what this book is all about.

Identity is the basis of your relationship with your users.

CHAPTER TWO

THE ECONOMIC IMPACT OF DIGITAL IDENTITY

In Chapter One we saw how identity has evolved from ancient times to our present digital age. In fact, the power of digital identity has grown to such a degree that **having a digital identity is rapidly coming to be seen in today's world as a fundamental human right** (more on that later in the chapter).

To understand this enormous power, just look at the governments around the world that are launching digital identity systems for their citizens and creating massive economic impact from it. According to research done by the World Bank, being able to streamline government services through a centralized digital identity solution can save on average 110 *billion* hours.[3]

---

[3] Olivia White et al., *Digital Identification: A Key to Inclusive Growth, Summary of Findings* (McKinsey Global Institute, January 2019), https://www.mckinsey.com/~/media/McKinsey/Featured%20Insights/Innovation/The%20value%20of%20digital%20ID%20for%20the%20global%20economy%20and%20society/MGI-Digital-identification-A-key-to-inclusive-growth.pdf.

Here's how these eGovernment services, as they're called, work: Say you want to pay a parking ticket, make sure you're up to date on your taxes, or connect with any other service that is run by a city, state, or federal government agency. When all such services are run through the same digital identity system—where citizens are identified by Social Security Number (SSN), Social Insurance Number (SIN), or the equivalent—it saves an incredible amount of time and money that in the past has been wasted by sending users to different places, with different logins, for each of their needs.

Billions of hours saved means *trillions* of dollars made. That's money for the government, of course, but it's also money for the tax-paying populace who can now utilize those funds in ways they like. Digital identity systems also make it that much simpler for the average citizen to access and navigate public services. Now, they only have to go to one central location for all their needs.

In the majority of developed countries like the US, Canada, or Germany, digital is already the name of the game for government services. But these mature economies face their own challenges: because so much of their digital landscape is already set up, it means they have to now gather extensive data from many different sources to bring it all under one digital umbrella. Connecting the dots between these different parties or government entities, as well as different states or regions, can be its own headache.

But in emerging markets like, say, Myanmar, the challenge is quite different: When it comes to public services, much of the important information and documentation still lives on paper.[4] The task for these countries is to build a whole digital ecosystem from the ground up.

---

4   Myanmar Centre for Responsible Business, "The Right to Privacy in the Digital Age: Experience from Myanmar," Office for the United Nations High Commissioner for Human Rights, June 4, 2022, https://www.ohchr.org/sites/default/files/documents/issues/digitalage/reportprivindigage2022/submissions/2022-09-06/CFI-RTP-Myanmar-Centre-Responsible-Business.pdf.

And because a lot of their services are still manual, there remains a great deal of payroll fraud. This makes sense: It is much easier for corruption of this kind to happen when identity is not validated and authenticated digitally. One study estimates that **transitioning to digital e-services could reduce payroll fraud around the globe to the tune of $1.6 trillion.**[5]

Given the enormous economic potential—which comes with reducing inefficiencies as well as waste due to fraud—it's no surprise that many developing economies are moving fast in the direction of establishing a central digital identity system.

In recent years, for example, India launched the world's biggest digital initiative to date, creating a centralized identity for each person—in a country of *well* over one billion! The system combines what's called an Aadhar number (like an SSN or SIN) with the biometric authentication of a fingerprint for every man, woman, and child.

5   White et al., *Digital Identification*.

The Aadhar card has now become the standard document for all identification purposes for over one billion Indians, and it is also being used to avail numerous government services that are linked to the unique identification number. For example, by adding it to a bank account, citizens can enjoy access to welfare payments and rations.

In China, there is something similar. Chinese citizens no longer need to carry a driver's license or any sort of physical ID. They just use their mobile wallet, where their digital identity is stored in an app. They can use this to access any of the public e-services.

Combined, this trend toward centralized government digital identity is creating a massive impact on the world economy. It is estimated that, under the India or China model, the nations of the world can reduce up to 90 percent of their current onboarding costs that are spent on gathering, verifying, validating, and authenticating information from their citizens.[6]

Of course, with all these public services going digital, the *people* also need digital identity more than ever.

A FUNDAMENTAL HUMAN RIGHT

In today's world, if someone doesn't have a digital identity, it means they are fundamentally deprived of important access to information, knowledge, and services. That is why digital identity has become so critical—and it is why we believe every human being has a right to one.

To deny someone a digital identity is to block crucial access to information and services—access that has become part and parcel of living a meaningful life in the twenty-first century.

---

6   White et al., *Digital Identification*.

> Centralized digital identity systems are having a major impact not only on the economies of the world but on each of our individual lives.

More and more, we are also seeing how digital identity is having an impact on *the private sector*. Going digital allows the company to be more productive and serve its customers more efficiently, putting out more products or services at lower costs. That reduced cost, in turn, helps consumers in the form of lower prices. Not only that, but shoppers can then use that money in other ways that are meaningful to them while simultaneously driving a variety of activities in the greater economy.

In Estonia, where a centralized eID (electronic identification) system has been implemented, each citizen can use their digital identity not only for public e-services but also in the commercial or business sector. This has saved the country lots of money and, according to Apolitical.co, boosted the GDP by 2 percent annually.[7]

In Estonia and other countries that have established these kinds of initiatives, we also see how their governments are trying to *educate* citizens around digital identity—selling them on all the features and benefits (e.g., not having to carry around physical documentation or store information in their head).

Finally, we see how these governments serve an important role as a bridge for the private sector. Now that citizens have digital identities to access their eGovernment services, there is the potential for businesses to connect with the same systems to help prevent fraud and other malicious activities.

---

7   Joel Burke, "e-ID Saves Estonia 2% of GDP a Year. It's Time America Caught Up," Apolitical Group Limited, December 7, 2018, https://apolitical.co/solution-articles/en/e-id-in-america.

WHAT COMES NEXT

As we've seen in this chapter, digital identity is critical for the world and every human. It has the potential to solve problems and drive progress both in our individual lives and our greater society and economy.

It is why you've come to this book: first, to understand the potential of digital identity, and then, to get serious about harnessing its power in your own organization and with your team and consumers.

Yes, identity—even in the digital space—has been around for a while, but management of customer identity through CIAM solutions is something relatively new, as we'll see in Chapter Three.

CHAPTER THREE

ENTERPRISE IAM VS. CUSTOMER IAM

If you are familiar with traditional IAM—which is all about the digital identity of your *employees*—you may think you know and understand CIAM. But as we mentioned in the Introduction, nothing could be further from the truth.

CIAM, of course, is not about the identity of the people who are part of your organization but rather your customers, a.k.a. external users.

These two solutions are entirely different beasts.

CIAM has only really been around since 2014—that's when third-party solutions came on the market—and even people in business and technology circles don't truly understand what it is. It's a huge challenge in our industry.

We get it: Terminology-wise, IAM and CIAM sound the same—they're both concerned with "identity and access management." They are both innovative approaches to restoring identity and restoring access information.

But the *kind* of information and the *way* to access and manage that information is completely different. The nature of the solution is entirely different and cannot be used for both types of identities.

> IAM and CIAM are separate products and must not be mixed up!

WHAT ARE THE DIFFERENTIATORS?

Let's dig a little deeper into this.

You already know that IAM is about internal and CIAM is about external identities. Internal means the company has full control over the users—employees—whose identities it's managing. External, of course, refers to the company's users, whom it has no control over.

With IAM, the company decides everything: when the employee's identity needs to be created and when it must be destroyed. The employee has no say. With CIAM, on the other hand, those choices belong with the user. They can change or update the details of their identity as they wish—they are in full control.

IAM is a centralized identity system. With CIAM, customer identities are decentralized.

There are other important differences too. For example, with IAM, data volume is fairly small. Even a big company of, say, half a million employees is small potatoes compared to the volume of identities managed by CIAM, where there can be 100 million, even 500 million users. Just think of Facebook, which has almost three billion monthly active users!

Same contrast when it comes to location. With IAM, an employee can access applications from all the different offices that a company owns. But even if the company has one hundred locations, it's still limited by geography. With CIAM, on the other hand, the consumer can use the web and mobile apps from anywhere in the world, as well as from any device.

To make this all as clear as possible, we have compiled Gartner's research findings outlining a comparison of the core features of CIAM and IAM:

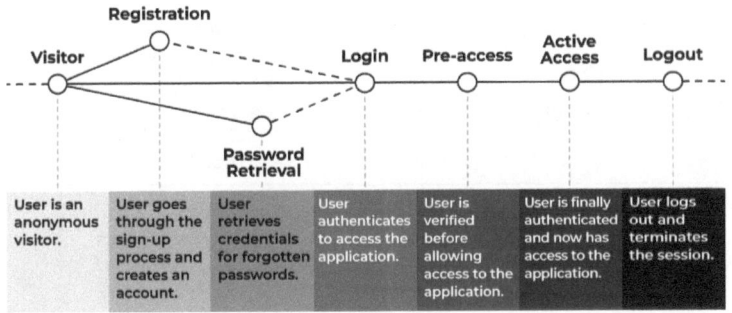

What are you supposed to make of these distinctions?

Well, the differences have big ramifications when it comes to security, experience, and privacy. With IAM, user privacy is minimal. The employer knows everything about the employee's identity. The government is still responsible under GDPR and similar regulations, which cover general data privacy rather than just customer data.

But with CIAM, of course, privacy is *everything*. And as we learned in the Introduction, privacy is a huge deal in today's world, which is why so many governments are developing and implementing privacy regulations.

Even from an engineering or infrastructure perspective, CIAM is way more labor-intensive than IAM. *Inside* a company, a system only needs to be up and running, for the most part, during business hours. Outside users, on the other hand, are signing into your platform 24/7, from anywhere on planet

Earth—which means you have to architect your product so that it's up and running all the time.

	EMPLOYEE IAM	CUSTOMER IAM
User	Employee is the user.	Customer (consumer) is the user.
Function	Works within an organization to manage employee access and permissions.	Works for external users, i.e., consumers, to create accounts and enable authorization across multiple web and mobile apps.
System type	Employee IAM is a centralized system where the organization controls and manages everything. Additionally, the user (employee) has very limited control.	Customer IAM is a decentralized system where control is with the user (customer). Customer decides when/if to create, authenticate, and delete an account and what device to use.
User Experience	There is no scope for the user experience. Employees have no choice but to use the system.	A great user experience is a must. If not, customers won't sign up, which will result in huge business losses.
User Privacy	There is no concept of privacy in Employee IAM systems as organizations' HR department stores employee PII as part of the employment agreement.	Consumer privacy is critical. Hence, the CIAM system is required to protect consumer privacy and comply with privacy laws such as GDPR and CCPA.
Financial Implication	It's a cost center. Not aimed at boosting revenue. IAM is implemented to strengthen security, improve internal operational efficiency, and achieve internal compliance standards.	This is a revenue center. Customer IAM aims to enhance lead generation, customer conversions, and engagement. It helps reduce support costs and increases operational efficiency and overall revenues.

	EMPLOYEE IAM	CUSTOMER IAM
Registration and Authentication Methods	Email login, employee identity number, phone number.	Email login, phone login, social login, passwordless login, one-time password (OTP) login, magic links, biometrics, etc.
System Scalability	Limited scalability required as most of the organizations don't have more than 50,000 employees.	System scalability is critical as organizations can easily have tens of millions of users.
Performance	Standard performance since employees within an organization are instructed and often trained to use it.	High performance is required since consumers have a low attention span and would not tolerate slow and broken systems. A slight lag in performance could affect key business metrics such as customer sign-up rates, return rates, and engagement rates.
Security	Employee IAM is a network security solution with limited exposure outside the network.	Customer IAM is a cybersecurity solution with exposure to the world wide web as customers may engage from any location, any device, and any time of the day.
Identity Store	Very basic data and credential storage.	Along with credentials, CIAM stores advanced data, including PII, activity, profile data, etc.
Integrations	Required to integrate with internal operation systems, such as HR, ERP, etc.	Required to integrate with customer relationship and service systems, such as customer relationship management (CRM), payments, loyalty, marketing platforms, etc.

You also need to have the infrastructure to serve users globally. This creates unique security concerns and considerations. Whereas IAM only has to worry about securing systems in certain office locations or from certain devices being accessed by employees, with CIAM you need to make your system available to the whole world. Anybody can access it. You can't control the location, the time, or what kind of device they are using.

Naturally, the security exposure with CIAM is on a whole different scale.

Finally, there is the **impact** of IAM versus CIAM. The former can really be considered a cost-saving or productivity-boosting product. It's fine for what it is. But CIAM has a much greater impact. Through CIAM, as we've learned, you drive revenue by attracting customers and by reducing churn and liabilities.

When it comes down to it, IAM is an information technology (IT) product. It's a tool that the IT department sets up and manages. CIAM, on the other hand, is a multidisciplinary product: The legal department, the security team, the product team, and the revenue team are all involved. Everyone plays a hand in the procurement of the CIAM technology.

CIAM has a much greater impact than employee IAM—it drives revenue by attracting customers and by reducing churn and liabilities.

WHAT THIS MEANS FOR YOU

Clearly, traditional IAM is just *not enough* anymore. The solutions that were initially created through IAM are woefully outdated and difficult to manage.

Especially if any of the following scenarios apply to you—and we suspect they do—then you *know* it's time to embrace a CIAM solution:

- Your application integration queue is growing faster than your team can support it.
- You have at least one business process that is currently outside of IAM control.
- Your legacy IAM vendor has failed to keep pace with changing technology, consumer requirements, and market trends.
- You don't want to be the next big data-breach headline.

In this chapter, we took the time to walk you through all the points of differentiation between IAM and CIAM to make our own point:

We know you are reading this book because you want to learn about management of customer identities. Not your employees. So, clearly you have to go the CIAM route instead of using the traditional IAM solution.

Seems obvious, but we still see people unsuccessfully trying to modify or tweak their IAM solution to fit the CIAM mold. Don't do that. Now that you understand why CIAM is a completely different play than IAM, one that answers a different need and value proposition, there's no reason for you to fall into the trap of using the same software.

WHAT COMES NEXT

Through the previous chapters about the evolution and impact of identity and this one about how CIAM differs from IAM, you've built your **foundation for understanding identity**. In summary, these chapters have given you the *what*: helped you understand *what* identity is and *what* CIAM is.

Now, in Part Two, we turn to the *why*: *why* digital identity poses such a problem and *why* it's mission-critical to do something about it!

PART TWO

THE CURRENT STATE AND OPPORTUNITY OF CONSUMER IDENTITY

CHAPTER FOUR

CONSUMER TRENDS AND KEY ISSUES

We all know that consumer attention span has dropped a great deal in the past few decades. The average consumer attention span is now only *eight seconds*—less than that of a goldfish![8] But you don't need us to tell you. You see it all around. Today's consumers are online, they're on mobile, and they want what they want at the drop of a hat. If you can't provide it for them, someone else will!

This wasn't always the case. But like more recent trends we will discuss in this chapter, the dwindling of consumer attention spans was something that had been building over time before it finally became a true game changer, sweeping the world and transforming the way people interact with brands.

Similarly, on the technology front, there was a time before large-scale adoption of smartphones when, of course, the

---

[8] Consumer Insights, Microsoft Canada, *Attention Spans* (Microsoft, Spring 2015), 6, https://dl.motamem.org/microsoft-attention-spans-research-report.pdf.

devices existed but weren't ubiquitous. But once this trend exploded, it transformed the market and revolutionized whole industries.

These two trends—the dwindling consumer attention span and the mass adoption of smartphones—are, of course, old news.

We bring them up here to make the bigger point that **consumer trends are critical**, and businesses that fail to pay close and consistent attention to which way the wind is blowing will inevitably find themselves in grave danger.

The new trends we are starting to see *now*, outlined in the following pages, will shape our world every bit as much as those of the past. They will certainly impact our businesses. As we've seen before, companies that evolve and adapt to the trends will survive and thrive. The rest will struggle and die.

> Understanding consumer trends is essential for any B2C business.

So, what *are* the biggest new consumer trends that you need to be aware of?

TREND #1: CONNECTED EXPERIENCE

Today's consumers expect a *connected* experience. That means they want to be able to start something on their mobile phone and then continue it where they left off when they get home and sit down at their desktop. Or when they're on the couch, they want to be able to return to the project using their tablet.

When it comes to *your* business, a **connected experience** means your users can interact with the same brand from multiple devices across multiple touchpoints and continue their interaction from any or all of them.

It means watching Netflix on a laptop and then finishing the movie on a smart TV. Or shopping for groceries on a phone while at work and then adding to the same cart from a home computer.

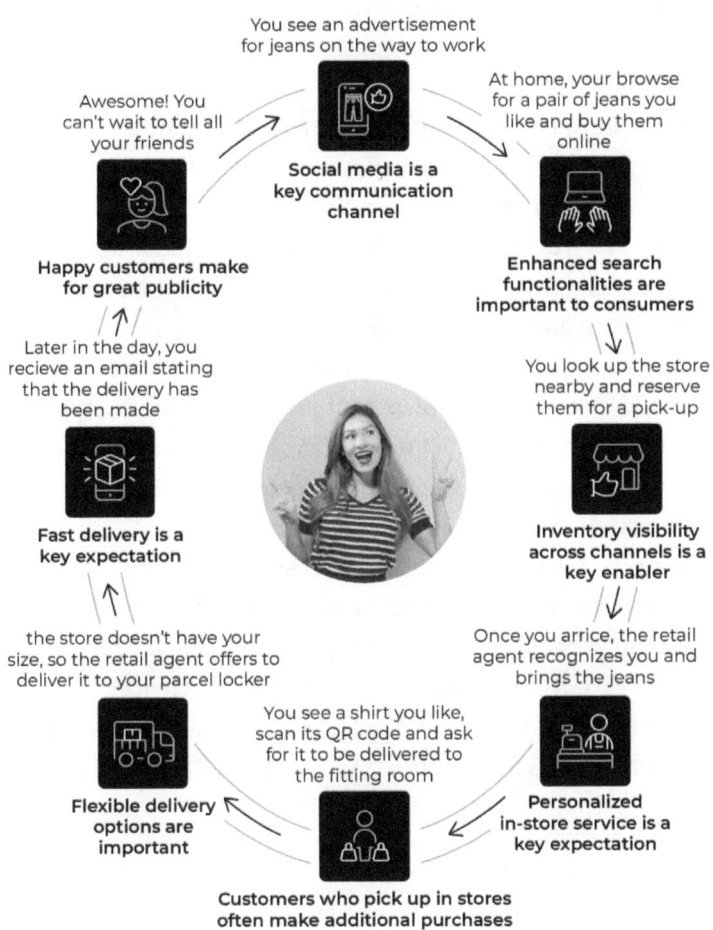

We can't stress this enough: A connective experience is a nonnegotiable in today's world. Consumers expect it from each and every brand they interact with. And it extends beyond their personal devices. Whether they're going to a call center or a brick-and-mortar store, they want consistency.

> Consumers don't want to have to reinvent the wheel every time they interact with a brand.

Data shows that not only do Americans spend an average of close to four hours on their smartphone every day, but 98 percent use multiple devices on the same day.[9]

This isn't true everywhere. In a country like India, and much of the developing world, it is common to *only* own a mobile phone. Not many people can afford a desktop or a smart TV. But in America and Europe, and most advanced economies around the world, people usually own multiple devices, and companies offer many ways to interact with them (web, mobile, store, etc.).

The connected experience has become a requirement for any business or brand worth their salt.

Within this trend, there are also sub-trends, for example the practice of buying something online and then picking it up in-person at the store. But it's all part of the bigger consumer trend of expecting a seamless, connected experience.

Think, for example, of Apple. When you go to their app store, whether it's on an iPhone, iPad, or MacBook, you get the

---

9 Laura Ceci, "Average Time Spent Daily on a Smartphone in the United States 2021," Statista, June 14, 2022, https://www.statista.com/statistics/1224510/time-spent-per-day-on-smartphone-us/; and Google, *The New Multi-Screen World: Understanding Cross-Platform Consumer Behavior* (Google, August 2012), https://services.google.com/fh/files/misc/multiscreenworld_final.pdf.

same experience. They recognize you and know your history. You are able to start from whatever point you left off.

One might even say that Apple is responsible for designing this whole concept of a connected experience. Certainly, the company was a pioneer—and the way they got ahead of this consumer trend is a great model for all of us.

TREND #2: PERSONALIZED EXPERIENCE

A *personalized* experience (or personalization) means designing your products or services to meet the unique needs and preferences of each individual customer. In today's world, companies are racing to offer more personalized experiences—because that's what we all expect.

What does a personalized experience look like? Say you're a sports fan and you go to wherever you get your sports news from. Your passion is basketball; that's what you care about more than anything. So, when you visit your favorite sports site, you want to be directed to the basketball stories. You don't want to have to wade through a bunch of headlines about soccer.

Similarly, if you're trying to rent a car from a website you've used in the past, and you've always rented SUVs from them, then instead of showing you two thousand different cars, a savvy company will personalize your experience by showing you the *right* cars.

Consumers want other elements from their personalized experiences too. According to a study done by Accenture, there are in fact **three things that customers expect brands to know about them personally: (1) their name, (2) their past, and (3) what they want.**[10]

---

10 "Consumers Welcome Personalized Offerings but Businesses Are Struggling to Deliver, Finds Accenture Interactive Personalization Research," Accenture, October 13, 2016, https://newsroom.accenture.com/news/2016/consumers-welcome-personalized-offerings-but-businesses-are-struggling-to-deliver-finds-accenture-interactive-personalization-research.

The same study shows that 56 percent would rather buy from a retailer that recognizes them by name. Seems like a small thing, but it connects the consumer with the brand. Sixty-five percent also prefer to buy from a retailer who knows their purchase history. Again, it drastically improves the experience when users don't have to browse through hundreds of shampoos to find the one shampoo that they buy every time. Which leads us to the final consumer expectation around personalization: 58 percent prefer to buy from a retailer that not only knows their history but specifically recommends options based on past purchases. This is where true personalization kicks in, using historical data to cater to the individual.

And like Apple in the earlier example, when it comes to personalized experience, the bar-setter in today's market is probably Amazon. When you buy something on Amazon, it knows your purchase history and gives you recommendations based on it. If you recently bought diapers, it would recommend related items for new parents.

This even goes beyond past purchases. Amazon maps the persona of the individual user with not only what they've bought but the city in which they live. Again, this is a subtrend within the bigger trend of personalization—it's called *localization.*

E-commerce retailers that take cues from Amazon and follow this same approach are getting it right and reaping the rewards: by using personalization and localization to recommend products, not only are they simplifying and improving the experience for their users but they're also increasing their own revenue.

Unfortunately, not every brand is as good at personalization as Amazon, and when a business *doesn't* do a good job, it means the consumer has to waste their time digging through a lot of stuff they consider irrelevant. Often, they will get frustrated and abandon the relationship with the brand altogether.

According to a 2019 survey by Gartner, brands risk losing 38 percent of customers because of poor marketing personalization efforts.[11]

It has only gotten worse since then.

> Failure to personalize is causing consumers to break up with brands left and right. It can be incredibly damaging to businesses.

TREND #3: CONTACTLESS EXPERIENCE

Prior to the COVID-19 crisis of 2020 and 2021, the trend of *contactless experience* with consumers was already picking up steam, but the global health crisis has accelerated it tremendously. Even in our digital age, at the end of the 2010s, there were still plenty of *non*-digital interactions. For example, if you wanted to get a business license, you might go to your city office or sign papers in person. There was a good chance you would have to come in contact with other humans.

But with the pandemic, by necessity many of these interactions became contactless. In both the public and private sector, organizations had to scramble to figure out how to serve their citizens and customers entirely through digital channels.

For example, pre-COVID, most people would go into Star-

---

[11] Gartner, "Gartner Survey Shows Brands Risk Losing 38 Percent of Customers Because of Poor Marketing Personalization Efforts," news release, March 11, 2019, https://www.gartner.com/en/newsroom/press-releases/2019-03-11-gartner-survey-shows-brands-risk-losing-38-percent-of.

bucks, line up to order, then wait in the store for a few minutes until the coffee was ready. But now, more and more customers are placing their orders through the Starbucks app. They don't have to wait in line or even worry about payment—the money is just deducted automatically from the app (which links to the person's bank or credit card).

Long story short: If consumers didn't already expect and demand contactless experience, they certainly do now. They don't want to have to meet anyone in-person when they are engaging with a brand. Or at least the trendline is moving rapidly in that direction. Maybe, for example, they want to be able to order their groceries online. Yes, if the store doesn't deliver, then most people are still willing to go pick up their order. But they don't want to have to spend a lot of time in the store shopping (and potentially risking their health).

We see this trend everywhere these days, from medicine to education to retail. Consumers are increasingly choosing to engage only with outfits that *get it* and offer a great contactless experience.

Brands that still cling to a traditional model of serving their customers may well offer top-notch service, but that alone doesn't cut it anymore. Which is why consumers are abandoning their relationships with those companies. The preference for contactless experience is undeniable and intensifying every single day.

TREND #4: VOICE-ACTIVATED EXPERIENCE

Beyond wanting contactless experiences rather than in-person, consumers are also moving rapidly toward *voice* as the interface of choice for interacting digitally with brands, and this is led primarily (at least for now) by smart speakers. According to Statista, 63 percent of American companies are investing in voice-enabled technology like Amazon Echo, Google Home, Apple Home Pad, and Sonos.[12] They are expecting that the number of digital voice assistants will reach 8.4 billion units by 2024.[13]

Moreover, what we're seeing is that once someone *starts* to use a smart speaker, the act of giving the machine questions and commands—"What's the weather today?," "What's the stock market news?," "Add this to my grocery list"—becomes more and more habitual. Not only is the number of users increasing but so is the amount of time they are spending using their smart speaker.

And with that increased use comes greater consumer expectations for *other* brands they may be interacting with. As a result, voice integration is fast becoming an essential component for apps.

Brands that fail to understand how much this trend of voice-activated experiences has picked up *already* need to get with the program and prepare themselves for what's coming. In the grocery space, for example, already 20 percent of every 100 million orders placed online are voice-based orders (i.e., come from voice alone). Maybe that doesn't seem like such a big number. But consider too that the voice-based shopping market is projected to reach USD 28.1 billion in 2032.[14]

---

12 Federica Laricchia, "Companies Developing Voice-Enabled Tech in the U.S. 2019, by Platform," Statista, February 14, 2022, https://www.statista.com/statistics/1134403/companies-developing-voice-enabled-tech-in-the-us-by-platform/.

13 Federica Laricchia, "Number of Digital Voice Assistants in Use Worldwide 2019–2024," Statista, May 22, 2024, https://www.statista.com/statistics/973815/worldwide-digital-voice-assistant-in-use/.

14 "Voice Based Shopping Market by Deployment Mode (On-Cloud, On-Premises/Embedded), Technology (Speech Recognition, Voice Recognition), Vertical (Retail, Atomotive, Healthcare, Education, other), and Region (North America, Europe, Asia Pacific, Middle East and Africa, and South America) Global Forecast 2022 to 2032," Adroit Market Research, accessed October 28, 2024, https://www.adroitmarketresearch.com/industry-reports/voice-based-shopping-market.

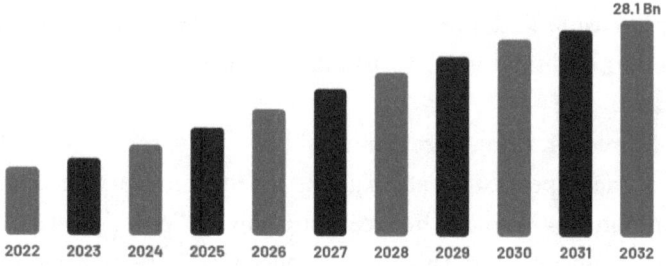

The Global Voice-Based Shopping Market 2022-2032 (USD Billion)

> *Voice* is fast becoming the preferred interface for consumers to interact with brands.

TREND #5: CONSUMER PRIVACY

Consumers have been rightfully concerned about privacy for a while now. It is what inspired landmark legislation like the EU's 2018 General Data Protection Regulation (GDPR)—a law that led to a tsunami of other privacy regulations around the world in the years that followed.

In 2020, there was the California Consumer Privacy Act (CCPA). In Brazil, the LGPD, the country's first ever general data protection law, went into effect in 2021. China introduced the Personal Information Protection Law (PIPL) in November 2021, setting stringent requirements on how its citizen's personal data is collected and processed. Thailand's Personal Data Protection Act (PDPA) came into force in June 2022, further exemplifying the region's commitment to data privacy.

Today, almost every country is working hard to introduce—or strengthen and expand existing—privacy laws.

What is driving these laws? With the advent of digital, lots of companies have had their data breached or been attacked by hackers. **It's become clear that governments need to step in to protect consumer information and push businesses to get serious about privacy.**

For their part, consumers themselves have also gotten wise to what's going on. On the consumer side, 70 percent of Americans say they are more concerned about their online privacy than they were just a few years ago.[15] In the EU, one in five agree with the statement that "businesses don't care about" their privacy. Clearly, there's a lack of trust: People just don't believe that businesses are doing everything necessary to protect consumer privacy.

Where is all this mistrust coming from? For one thing, in the past seven years or so, there have been many high-profile privacy breaches that have drawn significant attention in the media, creating a greater awareness of the issue. Companies like Facebook and Google, who operate on a truly massive scale, have come under scrutiny. And in some cases, hefty penalties or fines have been imposed.

Whatever the root of the public's misgivings in this area is, what it means for businesses is that they have been put on defense and now must struggle like never before to win (or win *back*) the trust of their consumers.

Once again, the businesses that succeed in this are the ones that will thrive and be able to both retain their customers and attract new ones.

---

15 Brooke Auxier et al., "Americans and Privacy: Concerned, Confused and Feeling Lack of Control over Their Personal Information," Pew Research Center, November 15, 2019, https://www.pewresearch.org/internet/2019/11/15/americans-and-privacy-concerned-confused-and-feeling-lack-of-control-over-their-personal-information/.

In summary, the privacy trend we've talked about here is actually twofold: On the one hand, it's about consumers' growing mistrust of businesses, and on the other, governments are pushing businesses to comply with privacy regulations.

TREND #6: SECURITY OF CONSUMER DATA AND ACCOUNTS

What is the difference between consumer *privacy* and consumer *security*? If the former—trend #5, which we just discussed—is largely about data and government regulation, the latter is about the nitty gritty of protecting consumer accounts (emails, passwords, credit card information, social security numbers, etc.).

Clearly the two are related. The connection can be seen, for example, in the alarming growth on the business side of fraud and phishing activity, social engineering attacks, and more. These are happening in companies big and small: Hackers attack a company's security apparatus and steal consumer information.

Sometimes, however, the threat to consumer data and accounts has nothing to do with hackers but rather the company itself sending consumer information to its partners in ways that are dishonest, negligent, or even illegal.

With both scenarios, consumers have become understandably concerned that their PII is being shared on the internet and that this sharing could be used to harm them in many ways after the initial privacy breach. They're hearing horror stories about accounts being hacked and people's money being stolen from their credit cards or bank accounts.

And they are right—these incidents *are* happening, and with greater frequency.

No wonder people are concerned about the security of their accounts, services, and information and don't feel safe providing their data. They have good reason to worry that companies will lose the data and compromise their personal information.

Ensuring that their customers' accounts stay secure remains a big problem for companies. What we're seeing in particular is that most businesses don't know how to properly secure *passwords*.

Sensitive consumer data introduces complex questions related to storing these details, what kind of encryption or hashing should be used to protect accounts, and what kind of access should be provided to customers—as well as internal employees—to see the data.

Way too many businesses are still not doing a good job at securing their customers' online accounts.

KEY ISSUES

These six consumer trends—connected experience, personalized experience, contactless experience, voice-activated experience, consumer privacy, and security of consumer data and accounts—are very real and widespread and are likely impacting *your* business. Moreover, because of them, we are seeing important new issues arise. In the following pages, we will explore **three key issues caused by these consumer trends**.

But first, now that you've learned a bit more about these trends, how are you supposed to know exactly what lessons to draw from them? How are you to understand which is most relevant to you and your business? For example, maybe contactless experience does not apply in your case, but voice activation is a big deal for you.

To figure out where your priorities should lie, you have to look closely at the distinct expectations around experience for your *own* consumers. Let's say you have a company that serves people over age fifty. It could well be that none of the trends and experiences we've talked about really apply to you at all. But if your business caters to consumers under thirty, you're probably in bad shape if you don't meet their new experience expectations.

How you and your business **meet the experience expectations of your customer** is one of the key issues facing companies today.

What's the answer? Businesses need to analyze their own consumer base to gauge its unique set of experience expectations. Are their customers asking for more contactless? Or do they care more about voice activation? Or both?

First, companies need to *understand* the expectations of their consumers, and then they can work toward *meeting* those expectations.

But meeting the experience expectations of the modern consumer is only one of the big issues caused by the trends we are seeing today.

With all the global regulations (GDPR, CCPA, etc.) cropping up these days—and then all the new security innovations and new ways of hacking into accounts—another key issue for businesses is how they **stay on top of all the security and privacy compliances** to protect the consumer.

Finally, whether we're talking about experience, security, or privacy, we know that all of these require continuous **technological innovation.** This means today's businesses have to invest in a lot of research and development, building new technologies and fostering ongoing innovation to make sure they stay on top of it all. If not, they will fail and be left behind in an ever more competitive landscape.

But first, they have to get their heads out of the sand and realize there's a problem.

> There are three key issues that have emerged from the new consumer trends: (1) meeting the experience expectations of the modern consumer, (2) staying on top of all the new security and privacy compliances needed to protect the consumer, and (3) keeping up to date with all the necessary technologies.

CHAPTER FIVE

REALIZING THERE'S A PROBLEM

Surrey, a municipality in metropolitan Vancouver, is the second largest city in British Columbia and one of the fastest growing cities in Canada. It's a diverse community that speaks more than one hundred different languages and welcomes a large number of new residents each month.

To accommodate this rapid growth, civic leaders needed to get creative in figuring out how to continue to provide excellent citizen services to the growing population. So, they created a digital platform called My Surrey.

In the past, Surrey residents had to use **different accounts to pay their parking tickets, register for swimming lessons, and other services.** They would use different passwords, webforms, or various PDF forms, and re-enter their data each time.

It was an all-too common experience, whether in government or the private sector: The user is required to sign up multiple times, and the applications don't talk to one another. It's a real mess, and we see it all the time. In business, it means every different business unit and application in a company has a different set of data on their end-users.

The data is not centralized but divided into different chunks in different databases.

It also means that businesses have to independently handle *security* and manage security practices and tools for each data store. Because the data is so spread out among different divisions, there can be no central security (or, for that matter, central privacy), resulting in significant operational inefficiency.

> How can a business make sure its data is secure when it's spread out in so many different buckets?

Clearly, decentralization leads to all sorts of privacy and security challenges—and even engineering challenges. How does the technical or IT team keep track of all the disparate information? In this environment, how can they manage who has access to what data?

Information access and access restriction is an ongoing concern among IT teams, as are the challenges (already discussed in Chapter Three) that come with having to manage and maintain infrastructure in different locations or countries, with different privacy laws.

But as we see with the example of the city of Surrey, it doesn't have to be this way. With its new portal, the city was able to consolidate all its services into one digital platform that allowed citizens to engage. The project took a great deal of vision: It was no small undertaking to gather all these complicated city processes and bring the whole range of municipal services online so that they could be easily accessible to everyone. The architects had to make sure all the key pieces were integrated, including some highly complex workflows.

It was worth it.

Since launched in 2019, it has been a great success—and a perfect example of how a unified identity solution can transform a broken user experience into something phenomenal. In fact, it is now being used as a model by other municipalities looking to effect similar transformations.

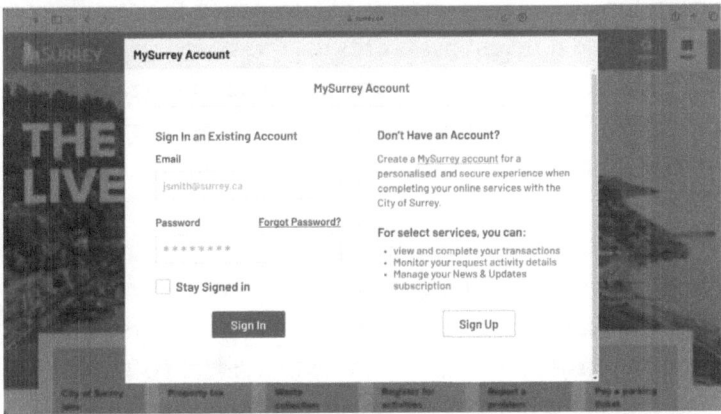

But this is only possible when organizations admit there is a problem and see the problem for what it is.

THE PROBLEM OF DECENTRALIZATION

The problem of decentralization manifests itself in a variety of ways and in lots of different situations. A company may see a dip in customer growth or customer retention. It may see less revenue coming in per customer or a higher cost of acquisition per customer. Vulnerabilities in some of its apps may be revealed.

These are all different outcomes of the same problem—and

it's a problem that can impact all organizations, from city governments to news media outlets to e-commerce sites. In the following pages, we delve into the various components of the decentralization problem and show how they are in fact all connected.

A BROKEN EXPERIENCE

First, there is the issue of **broken user experience**, which is what happened when residents of Surrey had to use different accounts and different passwords to access services. A broken experience is the result of requiring identity creation and authentication at multiple touchpoints where users interact with your brand (website, mobile app, tech support line, physical store).

As we've seen in earlier chapters, each of these touchpoints operate using different technology solutions. This means that users must identify themselves again and again. First, they go to your website, sign up, and create their identity. Then, they go to your store, only to find that no one there knows who they are. Then, they go to your app—or maybe the website of your other brand—and it's the same ordeal all over again.

The experience is *broken* because every time the user interacts with your brand, they have to re-identify themselves or create their identity again. It's not at all a unified, connected experience.

If you think this is far-fetched, think again. Step back and consider your own behavior as an end-user with the brands you interact with. Have you felt the frustration of having to sign up multiple times at different touchpoints? Have you gotten fed up because you can't remember if your password is the right one for whatever specific application you are using?

> If you're like most consumers in today's world, you've felt firsthand the pain of a decentralized user experience.

Thankfully, it doesn't have to be this way.

Take, for example, your Google ID, which you can use for Gmail, YouTube, Google Maps, Android Play Store, Google Photos, and in fact *all* Apple services. Users only need to create one identity, and then they can enjoy a unified experience. Not only that, but the experience is *personalized*. If a particular user happens to be a gamer, for example, when that person goes to the app store, they'll get recommendations for game apps. If they're a hip-hop fan, they'll see hip-hop suggestions in YouTube. And if a user already owns the latest Pixel phone, Google doesn't waste their time advertising it to them.

That is what a centralized, personalized user experience looks like, and it happens because the applications are actually talking to one another.

Not only is this a good thing for your consumer; it's good for your business. It means you don't have to do security ten times! It certainly makes privacy compliance a lot easier. You can have a dedicated team for a centralized identity system. It also eliminates the problem of the silo effect.

THE SILO EFFECT

Say you're a business owner or marketing leader and you're looking at all your digital properties, going over all your data. You realize your website has its own database of information about individual users. Even if your other touchpoints of locations share the same data, it's still split into three databases. That's called the **data silo problem.**

With bigger organizations, data can sometimes be split over dozens of databases. It's not just a problem of having these pieces of information in multiple places but also, frankly, not even knowing which data belongs to which user.

When these kinds of things happen, you wind up with what's called "orphaned data," which means data that has no owner. It is one of the most important concerns facing information technology practitioners. Without an owner, organizations experience difficulties managing—and when appropriate, removing—such data through its lifecycle.

> When it comes to removal of "orphan" consumer data, deleting it after a certain number of years (based on local jurisdiction) is a good start.

How does the data silo problem affect your business?

Well, for one thing, it prevents you from really being able to connect your data! With each individual end-user, you have a permanent silo effect throughout your organization.

When users create a unique identifier—whether an email address or some sort of account number—and they do this at, say, three different touchpoints, unknowingly they may be creating three separate digital identities. For the brand, this can cause a problem of **identity silos** inside the company.

In some cases, it's much worse. In addition to all the touchpoints we've already discussed, maybe you have a marketing tool like Marketo or a SalesForce CRM. These are all places where users need to create a unique identity as part of the packet of information that these platforms put together to define someone as a user.

Sometimes, in one organization, the same person can have twenty or even thirty digital identities!

> Digital interaction requires people to be identified digitally; there's no getting around that. But when users establish their unique identifiers at different touchpoints, often they unwittingly create multiple digital identities—which leads to identity silos within an organization.

DECENTRALIZED SECURITY AND PRIVACY

When it comes to data and identity, having information stored in all these different systems means your security team needs to possess and manage all the controls and compliances for each of the systems, and all the practices implemented on them.

The result is that security engineers and other security professionals are forced to repeat their efforts ad nauseam, across all these different places within the same company. They have to address encryption, using some sort of encryption algorithm, to stay government compliant. They have to address data access and how to control that access.

It's a big job to begin with, without having to do the same thing twenty times over! But that's what happens when **security efforts are not centralized**. The people in charge of security have to repeat the same security practices, controls, and accesses for all the different systems a company might have.

It's the same when it comes to privacy. Each and every company needs to ensure their end-users' privacy is not breached.

They also need to be compliant with privacy regulation not just at a local level but globally, depending on where the users are.

The lawyers in charge of this have a big job too. They have to work with the security team and engineers to make sure there are no privacy issues. With different privacy regulations in different countries, they also have to work across a lot of different systems. But because **privacy efforts are not centralized**, the attorneys end up—just like with the security folks—having to repeat their work across all these systems.

And it's not just about the different privacy policies for different locations; companies often have different policies for their users *at each touchpoint*. If you go to a website, you'll find one privacy statement, but then you'll go to one of the brand's other properties and find something else.

In the digital world, users give their consent, and companies have to capture that consent. But when the privacy language is different at each touchpoint, in essence you're requiring a separate legal package for each system.

When privacy efforts are not centralized, it can be very costly. You and your legal team may end up spending millions of hours (and paying exorbitantly for that time) just having to set up and maintain your system of privacy compliance.

INFRASTRUCTURE MANAGEMENT AND SCALING

Finally, with decentralization comes engineering problems. When a company does business in lots of different locations around the world, it becomes very difficult to manage that data and comply with all the different privacy regulations in the US, Canada, the EU, and elsewhere.

Not only that, but when you are operating twenty different systems, and they are running on twenty different servers in twenty different environments, the engineering manpower required is enormous. A company probably needs ten server engineers or dev-ops engineers just to manage those systems in all those different places.

We call this the **backend infrastructure management problem**.

And it's not the only problem when it comes to backend infrastructure: There is also the issue of **scaling**. Larger organizations have huge numbers of end-users, and these users are a global population. Take Nike, for example. Millions of people around the world want to interact with the Nike brand. In order to do this, the company has had to scale their infrastructure on a global level. This has meant building data centers in Europe, India, Asia, Brazil, throughout North America, and beyond.

With so many users, a company like Nike that is always scaling on a global level has to also scale its *systems* to support hundreds of millions of users.

This can become a big problem when you're spread across twenty different countries. To scale those disparate systems on a global level and serve users everywhere requires tremendous effort.

There's more to this problem than meets the eye. For example, different countries have different *events* that are unique to them. In the States, you might have a big cyber-sale going on for Black Friday. In Canada, there might be a promotion associated with a major sports event, like a hockey game.

As you can imagine, with these "peak-load" events going on around the world, it becomes very hard for a company's infrastructure to support it all.

> How much easier would it be for you to scale on a global level if you had one unified system?

EXERCISE #1

In this chapter, we've looked at the seven main problems associated with decentralization: broken user experience, data silos, identity silos, challenges with security efforts, challenges with privacy efforts, infrastructure management, and infrastructure scaling.

Now it's time to ask yourself: **How many of those seven problems is your organization currently facing?**

Maybe there's only one that resonates with you and the particular situation your company is in. That's great. In that case, you don't need to worry about the others.

But if you're looking at four, five, six, or even seven of these issues in your business, it should be a wake-up call. If there's one thing we want you to take away from this chapter, it's that these are *real* problems. They are what happens when identity is not centralized, when user experience is not centralized.

The sooner you realize this, the better positioned you'll be to correct your course.

As we'll learn shortly, when we get to Part Three, there is a single identity solution that can solve these problems. But first—no matter which of the seven problems you are facing—you must learn how to connect the dots and examine the root cause behind them all.

CHAPTER SIX

CONNECTING THE DOTS

By this point you're starting to see the contours of the problems that legacy digital identity strategies have introduced. You can probably even see it in your own personal life as a consumer. Maybe you bought something at a retail store the other day and wanted to have it shipped to your home. You already had an online account with the retail company, but they couldn't access it at the store, so they had to ask for all your information again: name, phone number, address, email.

It was especially frustrating because you knew everything was already entered in their system—your credit card information, billing address, all of it—but the system didn't connect.

As someone with a stake in identity issues within your own company, you probably see it from both sides. As annoying as it was to have to go through the whole process again when you were a customer at the clothing store, you knew what was happening behind the scenes. You knew that because the company maintained these different identity systems, they had to duplicate their efforts around security and privacy—and make sure your information was secure on their in-store terminal as well as their website.

You can likely relate to these problems. You have your own identity issues to deal with. Maybe **your company is losing revenue because your users keep abandoning their shopping carts.** Or maybe you had a security breach because you forgot some step on your twentieth database, and now your lawyers are saying the data leak has created a big privacy issue.

But hopefully you're now beginning to understand these problems a little differently. The more you learn about the issues surrounding digital identity, the more you see how the dots are connected—and how the problems you are experiencing around security, privacy, experience, and engineering all stem from the same *root cause*.

THE ROOT CAUSE

This is the point in your journey when you start to shift your whole mind-state and see the silo problems as part of the same bigger problem.

You come to understand that these different pieces of the puzzle are, in fact, all part of *identity*.

The train of thought goes something like this: First you see how data silos are causing your end-users to have a broken user experience and how these data silos are happening because of the identity silos. Then, you realize that because of these identity silos, you're not able to centralize your security and engineering efforts—and without centralized security efforts, you can't have privacy.

Clearly, **these problems are all connected. One feeds the next.** They cascade on one another—and to make matters worse, by having multiple systems, the implications of the problems are multiplied, sometimes by twenty-times or more.

But there is indeed a root cause behind it all—decentralization—and even if you don't know yet exactly what the solution looks like, you know it must address that root cause.

You know you can't solve the problem if you still have all

these different systems, built by different companies, that don't talk to each other. You can't solve the problem if you still have multiple systems, each with their own database. You can't solve the problem if your data and identity remain siloed. Or if you have a broken user experience. Or if your lawyers are working on privacy across a bunch of separate systems. Or if your engineers are bogged down trying to manage and scale the infrastructure separately for each of these systems.

By connecting the dots, you see that **at the center of it all are these separate, decentralized systems that don't talk to one another.**

Why is it so hard to get these systems to talk to one another?

It all has to do with technological restrictions. One of your systems might be built on PHP, another on Java, another on Watercrest. Maybe you're still using a legacy twenty-year-old point-of-sale system. It's not about the specific tech; it's about the fact that huge walls exist between these systems that are built in very different ways by different organizations with different philosophies.

> The root cause of all your digital identity problems is decentralization.

But there *is* a path out of this madness, as we will soon see in Part Three.

You are probably already starting to realize that what's needed is an underlying solution that is all-encompassing. You can't solve the data silo problem alone. You can't solve the privacy effort problem alone. There are no partial solutions. But because the CIAM solutions that you will soon encounter are aimed at the root cause, they are strategically designed to solve everything in one go.

Have we stoked your curiosity yet?

Stick with us. As you move through the following chapters, you will experience more of your own breakthroughs.

But first you must understand the full impact, the scope of the damage, these problems are *already* having on your business—so you can meet the situation with the urgency it demands and embrace the intensity.

CHAPTER SEVEN

UNDERSTANDING THE IMPACT

Are you aware of just how much your challenges around digital identity could be harming your business right now? Maybe so, but more likely not. One thing we can guarantee: By the end of this chapter, your eyes will be fully open to the devastating impact of these problems.

If it makes you feel any better, you're far from alone—the same issues are ravaging the industry.

Did you know, for example, that 86 percent of breaches are financially motivated?[16] Did you know that poorly managed privacy could result in a penalty in your European market to the tune of 4 percent of your global revenue?[17]

How about this one: Did you know that the average user

---

16   Verizon, *2020 Data Breach Investigations Report* (Verizon, 2020), 7, https://www.verizon.com/business/resources/reports/2020-data-breach-investigations-report.pdf.

17   "GDPR: Fines/Penalties," Intersoft Consulting, accessed May 10, 2023, https://gdpr-info.eu/issues/fines-penalties/.

attention span has dropped from 12 seconds to 8.25 seconds[18]—and because of that, if your page load speed is delayed by only one second, your conversion rate goes down by 7 percent?[19]

We've seen it firsthand: Businesses are losing their end-users left and right.

What about you? Are you losing users? How about your revenue? These aren't just minor concerns! If you're like the CIOs and CTOs we talk to every day, **your business is likely being affected to a much more severe degree than you realize—not just on the liability and risk side but also the growth and revenue side.**

In Chapter Five, we asked you to recognize the problem of identity silos for what it is. But here we call upon you to go further and understand the sheer *intensity* of the problem. We use this word deliberately: A lot of people know they have this problem but don't know just how serious it is.

Within any organization, it can be hard to see the forest for the trees. Say an engineering problem has arisen. When the security team looks at it, they see a security problem. When the folks who oversee revenue look at it, they see an experience problem. And so on and so forth.

We want to help you take a broader view and see the problem from all sides so that you can understand its intensity and **recognize the massive implications across departments, well beyond what you and your company previously believed.**

We know it's hard to face the truth sometimes. But when

---

18 "Average Human Attention Span (Statistics)," Golden Steps ABA, October 21, 2024, https://www.goldenstepsaba.com/resources/average-attention-span.

19 Alex O'Byrne, "A 1 Second Delay on Your Page Load Can Cause a 7% Reduction in Conversions. How Do You Solve It?" *We Make Websites* (blog), February 22, 2023, https://www.wemakewebsites.com/blog/improve-page-load-speed-increase-conversion.

you see the actual numbers, the impact in dollars and cents, the truth becomes impossible to ignore.

> Are you losing users? Are you losing revenue?

People are scared out there, and rightfully so. The recent history of identity is littered with cautionary tales that will put the fear of God in you.

For example, there's a computer company in Canada that keeps all its customer identity information unencrypted on a server. When the business went bankrupt, the server was auctioned off in the bankruptcy sale. Just think about how much confidential customer data—including credit card numbers—must have been leaked. Terrible! As for the company, not only were they exposed to a lot of ridicule, but also possible legal action.

That's a particularly egregious example, but what we see more often is that companies are relatively aware of the dangers when it comes to the liability and risk side of their business but **take their eye off the ball with growth and revenue.** We've already seen how a clunky sign-on experience can nibble away at profits. We've seen how brands leave good money on the table by not centralizing their systems.

Along the same lines, it's not unusual for companies to spend millions of dollars in marketing around peak events like Black Friday, only to see that money go to waste because their mobile app couldn't handle the volume of users.

In the US, the Obama administration had a similar digital identity issue in launching its website for the Affordable Care Act. The system failed because it couldn't handle the load on the infrastructure and system scaling.

In fact, each of the seven digital identity problems outlined in Chapter Five (broken user experience, digital silos, identity silos, decentralized security efforts, decentralized privacy efforts, infrastructure management, and infrastructure scaling) **can turn into major threats to your business.**

Each one of these has its own profound implications—for specific departments and teams, as well as your organization as a whole.

UNDERSTANDING THE POTENTIAL DAMAGE

When you look at the destructive effects of these different problems, you can see how one cascades into another and amplifies the pain.

A broken user experience affects not only user satisfaction but also the company's conversion rate (how well it converts traffic into customers). Same with retention rate—turnover rises, as does the cost to acquire new users.

In fact, when it comes to a bad user experience, virtually *everything* is negatively impacted. Even a (seemingly) small snag can have a snowball effect, with massive repercussions among departments of a company: the revenue team, security, marketing, and more.

> Each of the seven main problems around digital identity has its own serious implications.

It doesn't make life any easier that standards and expectations among consumers today have become so high. People have endless options, and they interact with many different companies—some of which, it must be said, are at the forefront when it comes to solving these identity problems.

This means that **users are having fantastic experiences with some providers and really bad ones with others.** If you wind up in the latter category, you're toast.

Similarly, when you have data silos and identity silos, it limits your ability to upsell and cross-sell to your end-users. *You're missing out on revenue.* Think about a company like Vogue: they have *Vogue* magazine, *GQ*, and a few others. If you sign up online with Vogue and are browsing on their site, they will start throwing you relevant content from *GQ*. You are then able to click on that and spend time on *GQ*'s site. But, of course, you can't enable such experiences as a brand when your data and identity are separated in silos.

Moreover, when your data is broken, it becomes much harder to make informed strategy decisions. Because of your data silo problem, you're just not properly situated to look strategically at the overall landscape of your business and make important choices and conclusions around your users, revenue, growth, and positioning.

Sounds grim? We know. But **these aren't just scary thoughts. There are specific metrics associated with each of the problems**, and the numbers tell the story: These issues around identity are costing you and your company money, causing you to lose revenue.

If there is a security breach or privacy issue, for example, the metrics will reveal the extraordinarily high costs of resolving the problem. Not only will you be handed a lawsuit, dragged to court by your end-users, and required to spend millions of dollars in fees and penalties—but of course your brand will also be significantly weakened.

To add insult to injury, the chances of you getting in hot

water over a security breach is substantially higher *because* your security efforts are not centralized. That is why it's so dangerous to operate and manage your customer data and security practices across so many systems: The chances of somebody breaching is very high. You'll also have to spend that much more time and money to get all your compliances and certifications in place.

Even among your internal employees, the risks associated with their access are higher when security efforts are decentralized.

What about your privacy efforts? How much is it costing you to not have them centralized? As we learned in Chapter Five, the legal costs will quickly spiral out of control when your legal team is spending so many hours managing privacy statements and privacy acceptance among disparate users and across systems, platforms, and locales.

More important, **the chances of a privacy breach greatly increase when privacy efforts are scattered rather than centralized.** Like with a security breach, you may also have to go to court—and with twenty different systems, you'll need ten pricey lawyers (at least!) just to manage it all.

Wouldn't you rather have (and only have to pay) one primary attorney, who dictates the company-wide privacy statement?

Finally, consider the massive costs of infrastructure management. If you're working from a number of different servers (one on AWS, one on Azure, one on your on-premises, in-house server), it means you're likely paying through the nose for all those engineers needed to manage the servers.

Not only does that become very complicated, but it also makes it virtually impossible to scale—because **the costs are so high trying to scale twenty different systems instead of one.**

It can be a complete disaster. Try having two million people suddenly clamoring to access your sale offering, only to see the login systems fail because of your company's poor approach to backend identity infrastructure scaling.

What ends up happening in that scenario is that you actually come full circle and wind up back at the broken user experience. In effect, you *acquired* that bad experience, damaging your own sales activity and revenue in the process.

WHAT COMES NEXT

In all these examples, the case is pretty clear. When you look into how much you're spending—all the resources, human and financial, that you're pouring into these areas—it becomes **virtually impossible to justify *not* pursuing a centralized identity system, a.k.a. a CIAM solution.**

Which brings us to Part Three.

In the past four chapters, you've come to understand the various problems associated with digital identity, how they're related, and how badly they are likely affecting your business. Along the way, you have learned to take a broader view of these identity issues and *why* they are happening. Now, in the following chapters, we will look, finally, at the *how*: how to use CIAM solutions to leverage the power of digital identity and solve these problems once and for all.

Ultimately, not only will you turn around all these damaging forces that have been hurting your brand, but you will also transform your users' experience and win their trust like never before.

PART THREE

STRATEGY AND DEVELOPMENT OF YOUR CIAM PROGRAM

CHAPTER EIGHT

STRATEGIZING A CIAM SOLUTION AND IDENTIFYING THE PIECES

Do you ever notice that when you go to Google, you only have one username and password? It doesn't matter if you're on Google.com or Gmail or Google News or even YouTube. You log in once and you can access everything.

With Google and its associated properties, **you only have one identity.** Sure, you may have two different Gmail accounts, but that's a specific choice on your part—and Google makes it very easy to switch between accounts.

In terms of identity, and all the digital challenges we talk about in this book, Google is a shining example of how to do things *right*. They create a unified experience, and anyone who's ever used Google can attest to this. Of course, most of them have never heard of CIAM, but they can *feel* it when they interact with Google and when they access YouTube and the Android app store using the same account. Through their digital journeys, the login process is seamless, without any of the usual frustrations.

That is CIAM in action.

What's in it for Google? Why do they do it this way? Certainly, they have their own business angles and benefits. Now that they know, for example, you like to watch gaming videos on YouTube, the next time you go to their app store, they can showcase games for you to download.

By using information and identity to cross-sell and upsell to their users, Google significantly raises their revenue per user.

But it's more than that too. The unified experience—of being able to use the same identity to access everything—creates loyalty and engagement.

Wouldn't you want the same for your application?

You would. And turns out, you can.

YOUR CIAM STRATEGY

You too can have a system that lets your users create their identity in one place and use the same identity to interact anywhere with the brand.

Unlike many of the examples we've seen in this book, with a CIAM solution, your users will be able to deploy that single identity, single username and password, through a single login system. They will then have a single backend profile that creates a smooth experience for them across your company every time they interact with you.

Through CIAM, broken experience is converted into unified experience. Identity silos and data silos are converted into single identities and single user profiles. Decentralized security—that needs to be managed at ten different places—is converted into centralized security.

Privacy regulations that need to be managed across ten different brands are centralized across an augmentation network. Painful management of distributed engineering infrastructure is replaced by technology.

CIAM means:

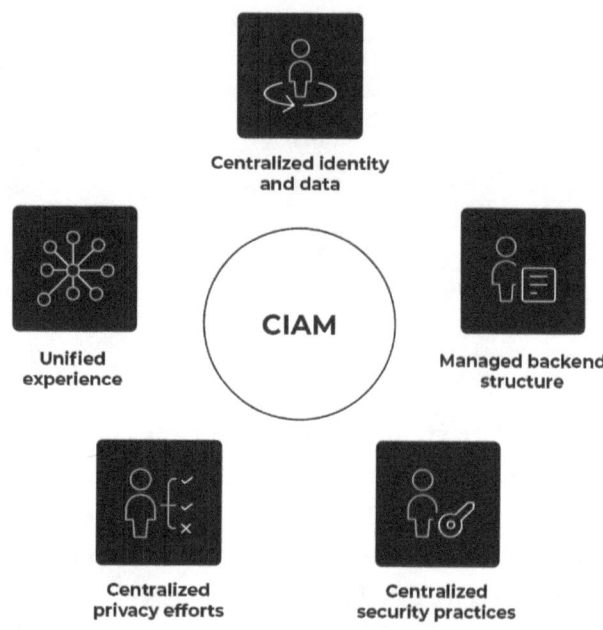

1. **Unified experience:** By creating a single identity and enabling single sign-on capabilities, CIAM allows you to create a unified experience across all your user touchpoints.
2. **Centralized identity and data:** CIAM lets you have identity and data in a single place, a database connected to all your applications, giving you a unified snapshot of each individual user.
3. **Centralized security practices or efforts:** Only through CIAM can your security team monitor account security, data security, and other activities all in *one place*.
4. **Centralized privacy efforts:** By centralizing identity and data through CIAM, you can now have a company-wide

privacy statement, privacy practices and policies, as well as built-in technological capabilities to ensure all government regulations are fulfilled.
5. **Managed backend infrastructure:** By centralizing through CIAM, you can manage your database, data backup, server, and more *through the technology itself*, which frees up your engineering team.

Now that you are developing a deeper understanding of the CIAM solution, **you should already be thinking and formulating your strategy for how to deploy it in your company.** Which are the departments you're going to need to talk to? What information will you have to gather from them?

In the past, each department and team (engineering team, business team, etc.) has had these different challenges but didn't know how to solve them—because they weren't seeing how everything fit together.

Knowing what you know now about CIAM, you are well positioned to *identify the pieces.*

IDENTIFYING THE PIECES

What do we mean by identifying the pieces?

Let's use the example of one of our clients. They knew they had an identity problem. It was a drawback they had seen across departments with their marketing team, security team, engineering team, and legal team.

They had been **experiencing the damaging effects of identity fragmentation** and wanted to figure out how to centralize their security and privacy efforts.

This company operated in three countries and had two separate brands. So, first, they set out to have a better grasp of all their user touchpoints. What they discovered was that users were touching both their brand sites, each with three versions for each country, and then also through their support system at their call center.

Next, they asked themselves, were these touchpoints on the backend really all on the same applications? The answer was no. It turned out, three of their websites ran on the same database, but a different (older) system was used for the rest of the sites.

Before long, this company found themselves in a much better position to solve their problems. Having gone through the process outlined above, they were **finally able to understand their backend databases and how exactly the site loads were broken down.**

But that was only possible because they had done their internal research, gathered the necessary information, and followed a clear methodology to identify what was really going on in their organization.

> Do the touchpoints on your backend run on the same applications?

In this chapter, we will share with you all the specific steps of our **methodology for identifying the pieces**—so you too can gain clarity on the problems you're seeing in the different divisions and departments of your company, as well as the different regions and brands.

We will also show you exactly what **questions** to ask in order to get to the bottom of these problems.

Just like our client, you will learn how to do your internal research and go deep with your inquiries, looking specifically at issues like whether the touchpoints on your backend are the same application or different applications and how your site loads are broken down.

But it all begins with taking an initial inventory of your user touchpoints.

EXERCISE #2

There are all sorts of ways that a user can interact with a business or organization. These touchpoints include: web, mobile, telephone, in-person, kiosk, advertisements, point-of-sale, chatbot, Internet of Things (IoT), and smart speakers.

Take the time now to identify all *your* customer touchpoints. Where are your users interacting with your company? What are all the ways the two parties in this relationship—business and consumer—are touching each other?

Make a list and try to map out these touchpoints within your digital ecosystem.

Done? How did that feel?

Let's keep going.

In the following pages, we will outline what we've seen to be a very crisp, effective methodology for identifying the pieces. Trust us: These steps really *work*.

METHODOLOGY FOR UNCOVERING PROBLEMS

How do you find out what's really going on, internally, in your company? How do you go about uncovering the problems?

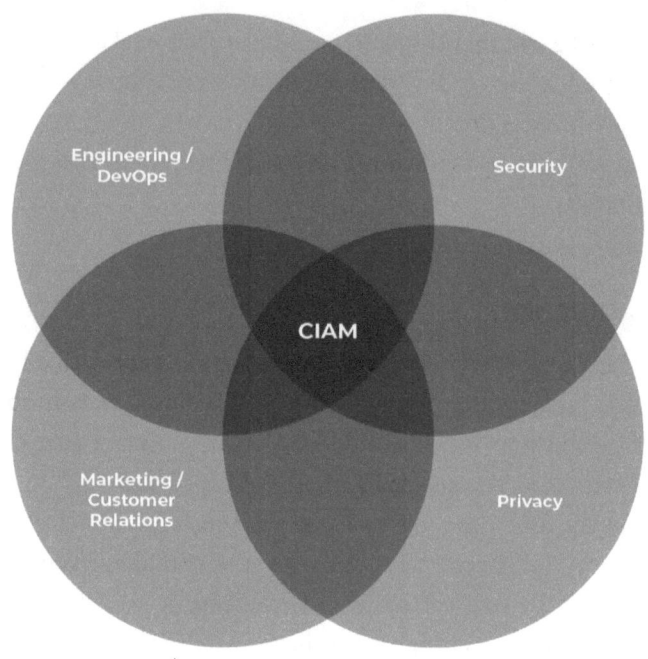

The first step is to **identify all the individuals and divisions involved.** Who are the leaders and teams that are working on user identity, user data, and/or user experience? It may sound obvious, but you need to know your territory. You can't find the problems if you don't know where to look. So first things first, you have to define the domain within which the problems lie.

Next, you also need to **map the *systems* that align with those people** whom you've now identified. Think of it this way: You already know the three areas you're concerned with, which are identity, data, and experience. You already know the key people responsible. Now you just need to know—on a systems level—which are the systems in play with those individuals.

Once you've done that, you can **start speaking with personnel responsible** for those areas and those systems and interview them about the issues and challenges they're facing. At this point, your questions will be open-ended: What are the initiatives they are taking around identity, data, and experience? And most importantly, *how* are they conducting these efforts? Depending on the responses you get, you can start digging deeper.

For example, if you ask a team leader how they do a particular thing, and their answer is "I go to engineering manager one, then I go to engineering manager two…then I go to engineering manager ten," that's a red flag that there is likely a problem. Which means it's time for the next step, which is to **dig into the data**. How many hours were spent going to those ten engineers? How many days did it take to create the new policy? Data helps you understand the impact these problems might be having on your business.

But you can't get the full picture if you only hear one side of a story, or one piece of a puzzle. Now that you know what the one fellow is saying, you should talk to someone else. How about your head of legal—what is her take on the situation? What about marketing? It is quite common that one individual will voice a problem, and another doesn't see it as a problem whatsoever. This is why it's so important to draw data from a variety of sources. You're going to want to talk to everyone you've identified as involved.

Make sure you're getting the *full* story, from all angles, about the digital identity issues within your company.

WHAT QUESTIONS TO ASK

There are a number of questions **every company needs to ask itself**. As a leader, you may already feel like you have answers to a lot of these. But you should still go out and talk to your people, look at the data, and try to uncover these problems. To implement your CIAM solution, you're going to need to have the full spectrum of information.

With **legal**, the two most important questions are: How are we ensuring that we are complying with government regulations, and how are we effectively and truthfully deploying or implementing our legal practices among our users?

What about your **security** division? How are they working to protect your customers' identity and accounts? Do users need multifactor authentication (MFA) to protect their accounts? Is there encryption or hashing for user data? Who is responsible for securing the data? Are security efforts being duplicated because of data silos? How is the security team ensuring that they are adopting the latest, best practices in the identity industry and staying ahead of the curve? How are they working with the legal team to be certain that the company is compliant with security regulations? And if privacy or security violations were to occur, what would the impact be—what is their assessment of the risk?

Next, go to your **engineering** team and interact with them. How are they managing your customers' identity and data in the backend? How are they ensuring a high-performance experience for your user (i.e., peak loads, latency, and workflow performances)? What are they doing to maintain the customer registration and authentication system? What resources are they putting toward maintaining this system in terms of engineering time and budget—and is there a better use of these resources than what they're doing right now?

What about your **marketing and business** teams? How are they using existing customer data to understand your target market? How well *do* they understand that target market? Do they have a holistic view of who your users are? Would having a centralized view of all your user data help with upselling and cross-selling strategy and campaigns? How efficient are their current marketing strategies in driving results?

Then comes the **customer experience** team. Ask them: Are users having difficulty registering and logging into accounts? What are the most common complaints they're hearing from users about their accounts? What's the process for reporting these issues? Specifically, what's the process for helping users with account access issues, such as forgotten passwords, login/registration, and profile management? Are users able to easily manage their profiles and preferences through their accounts?

Finally, ask your **data** teams: How many databases do they use for user data? Who is responsible for those databases? What other systems or tools do they use to host this data (marketing automation, CRM, DMP)? How many unique users do they see? What kinds of user data are they storing? And do they have a way to clearly answer those questions?

We know these might seem like a lot of questions, but it's essential that you be *thorough* and *precise* in order to get the answers that you need.

Talk to your people. Ask them about the problems they're encountering.

What next?

Now that you've gone through the process of asking questions, doing internal research, and identifying the pieces of the problem across departments, locations, and brands, you are ready to take everything that you've uncovered and strategically apply CIAM solutions to your organization.

You're ready to create your own architecture.

CHAPTER NINE

CIAM REFERENCE ARCHITECTURE

Now that you understand the concept of CIAM and have identified the unique pieces of your organization's problem around digital identity, how are you going to put it all together and *apply* everything you've learned? How are you going to deploy and implement a strategy to bring these CIAM principles to your business?

It all begins with what we call the application **framework**. This is a one-page summary that you put together and will ultimately use to present to the necessary decision-makers.

The idea here is to take what you identified from the exercises in the previous chapter and synthesize that information into this common framework or canvas.

If the goal of CIAM is to *centralize*—to bring together brands, subsidiaries, websites, data, and more—the application framework shows *where* to apply this centralizing approach, based on your category or categories of problems.

In particular, it helps you figure out which of your brands you can **bundle** and pull together into the same entity.

But first, we must understand how CIAM fits into the bigger digital ecosystem and break it down into its constituent parts.

OVERVIEW OF CIAM ARCHITECTURE

The function of CIAM within a digital ecosystem is to connect identity with external online applications and then feed that information into business applications, such as analytics, marketing, commerce, and content, as you'll see in the following diagram.

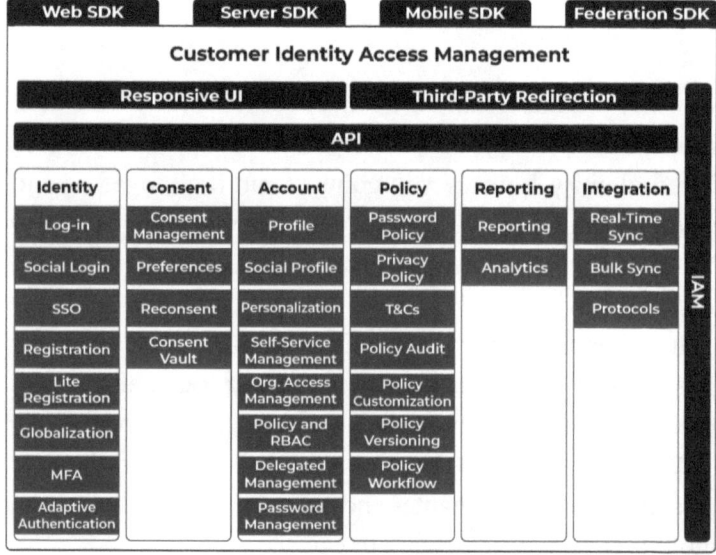

In addition to the business applications listed on the far right, the diagram shows the **six components of CIAM architecture: identity, account, policy, privacy consent, reporting, and integration.**

Let's look at these one by one:

I: IDENTITY

Identity—the first component of CIAM architecture—is about using the consumer's online profile to capture identifying details about them. Identity is created in the system after initial registration, which can either be done manually by filling out a registration form or by using social login (or something called lite registration, which will be explained below) to capture information from social media.

It is important to note that consumer identities may vary based on the region and local regulation.

Then, within this first component of CIAM architecture—identity—we find eight sub-components:

1. **Login:** This is the method of authenticating a user and is sometimes used to unlock functionality that is only available to authenticated users.
2. **Social Login:** Also known as *federated* login, whereby a user identifies themselves through a third-party site.
3. **Registration:** This step is what makes it possible to create an identity for a specific service, website, or app.
4. **Passwordless Login:** The process of verifying a user's identity with something other than a password, like a temporary verification link.
5. **Phone Login:** Users can enter their phone number as a username, and they will receive an OTP on their phone with which they can log in.
6. **No Registration:** Sometimes the rest of a registration can be completed later, and only what's called a minimum viable identity is used initially. But additional site functional-

ity may be dependent on providing further registration details.
7. **Single Sign-On (SSO):** Here, users just log in directly to multiple websites or applications with a single set of credentials.
8. **Localization:** This is what makes it possible to register, authenticate, and manage identities in different countries while still conforming to local standards and regulations.

Once the identity is created and verified, it is imperative that a profile be built to identify and validate the consumer during the next authentication. Which brings us to the second component of CIAM architecture:

II: ACCOUNT MANAGEMENT & SECURITY

The account profile is built from consumer account data and can contain items such as social profile data, personal information, policy and roles data, and more.

Consumers can directly manage their profile data, policy, and security settings, as well as their password policy. They can even do a self-service password reset. This is all crucial in today's consumer-facing era. **Account management is self-service.**

Then, within this second component of CIAM architecture—account—again we find ten sub-components:

1. **Profile:** The descriptive information that you collect about customers (must be configurable).
2. **Social Profile:** This is what makes it possible to incorporate profile data from social platforms.
3. **Personalization:** This is what makes it possible to hold wider data sets across channels.

4. **Organization Access Management:** This allows accounts to be managed at the customer organization level.
5. **Policy and Role-Based Access Control:** This allows access to resources to be controlled at the level of individual roles and/or through policies (by modeling roles and organizational policies).
6. **Delegated Management:** This gives the ability to define groups and roles in which profile management is delegated to customer administrators.
7. **Password Management:** This gives the ability to "self-serve" forgotten passwords or to change passwords.
8. **Self-Service Management:** This allows the profile's owner to continue to make changes.
9. **Multifactor Authorization (MFA):** This means that more than one factor (a one-time password, for instance) is used to authenticate.
10. **Adaptive Authentication:** This is what makes it possible to assess risk around identity, balancing security concerns with the goal of a frictionless experience.

Then, within the consumer account, multiple *policies* are needed to manage the privacy and security of the account profile, which brings us to the third component of CIAM architecture:

III: POLICY

Password policy is what dictates the security of the account. But in addition to passwords, there are a number of other important policies: privacy, terms and conditions, audit, customization, versioning, and workflow for the account. Let's take these one by one:

1. **Password Policy:** This gives the ability to define rules for acceptable passwords and how long a password can remain valid before it needs to be changed.
2. **Privacy Policy:** Not only is this the vehicle for configuring the rules around privacy that customers will be asked to accept, but it also holds responsibility for full auditing of the policy versioning and tracking changes.
3. **Terms and Conditions Policy:** This is where the terms and conditions that customers have to accept upon registration are managed.
4. **Audit Policy:** Actions performed by administrators and users must be logged, with an eye toward policy changes and failures.
5. **Policy Customization:** This allows policies to be extended or specialized for sites that children frequent.
6. **Policy Versioning:** This allows for tracking of all policy revisions.
7. **Policy Workflow:** This allows specifically for tracking of different versions of policies for different customers, as well as re-consenting workflows and actions triggered by significant changes to policies.

Policy is one thing, but then users must formally approve of how their profile is to be accessed, which brings us to the fourth component of CIAM architecture:

IV: PRIVACY & CONSENT

Privacy and consent management is the process for recording the user's approval, as well as their communication preferences. They can enable or disable the consent settings about communication, account access, account deletion, and more.

Privacy and consent also encompass the full auditing of consent versioning and tracking of policy changes.

Then, within this fourth component of CIAM architecture—privacy and consent—we find five sub-components:

1. **Consent Management:** This not only allows customer consent to be recorded but also enables customers to withdraw their consent.
2. **Communication Preferences:** With this, customers can configure and reconfigure how they'd like to receive messages or opt in or out of various communication channels.
3. **Re-Consent:** This defines the chosen time period after which it is necessary for customers to reconfirm consent.
4. **Consent Vault:** This is where consent is stored for each version of one's policies.
5. **Privacy Regulations:** Compliance laws from around the world like the EU's GDPR and California's CCPA dictate how organizations should meet the regulatory requirements for collecting, processing, and maintaining personal data in a country.

V: REPORTING

The fifth component of CIAM architecture—reporting—is incredibly important, as it is the vehicle for providing all detailed information about the user's identity, behavior, engagement, and consent to security and privacy policies.

Under this category of reporting, there are three sub-components:

1. **Administration Portal:** This allows for the creation, management, and searching of individual consumer accounts in CIAM.

2. **Reporting:** This allows for the generation of reports on the use of CIAM.
3. **Analytics:** This allows for data to be collected on customer interaction with CIAM.

VI: INTEGRATION

The sixth and final component of CIAM architecture is key: *Integration* is what takes care of syncing consumer account data from CIAM to third-party tools used by other business units, such as analytics, marketing, commerce, and advertising.

This synchronization between third-party tools and the CIAM account data also must be *two-way*. This allows for a centralized view of the data, which is needed to maintain consistency and privacy.

Finally, within this sixth component of CIAM architecture—integration—we find three sub-components:

1. **Real-Time Sync:** This allows for syncing of identity data (including consents) to other systems that require such data.
2. **Bulk Sync:** This allows for syncing of a *bulk volume* of identity data (including consents) to other systems that require such data.
3. **Protocols:** This refers to the enduring support and attention required for the protocols by which identities and authentication are shared.

EXERCISE #3—YOUR FRAMEWORK

Now, in preparation for creating your own CIAM architecture, it is time to put together *your one-page application framework*.

To get you started, we have designed the following chart,

which will help you understand how user identities can be grouped and managed within your organization.

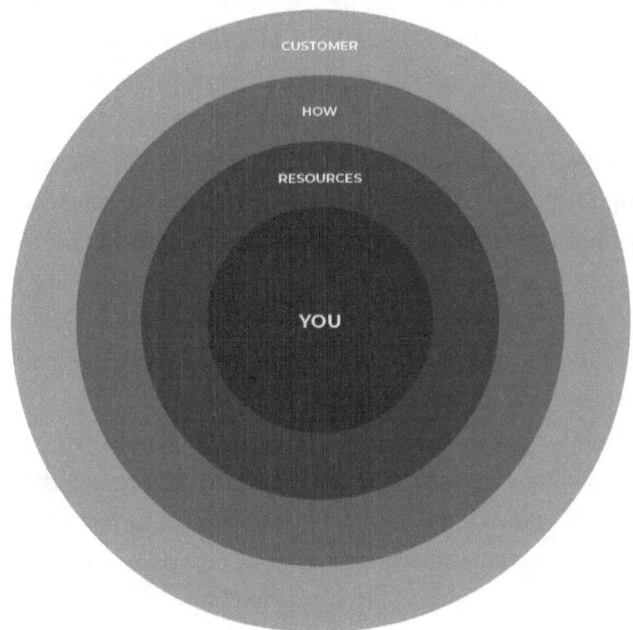

Everything in the framework revolves around **you and your corporation.** By that, we mean the top-level (parent) company as well as all the subsidiaries, divisions, and legal entities that make up its overall structure. This also includes all the countries where your company operates and/or has users and all the distinct brands that belong to it.

Begin by entering this information into your framework. Make sure to clarify which brands belong to which business units.

Then, look beyond this inner circle to your **resources:** What are the internal teams involved in managing user identity? Go ahead and enter these into your framework now as well. Possible answers include legal, engineering, marketing and business, security, customer experience, and data and identity.

Next, panning out to the next layer in this model, we get to what we call **the *how*** — i.e., how you interact with your users. First, you'll want to add to your framework all the digital properties you use, including all customer-facing websites, mobile apps, kiosks, and chat programs. Second, you'll list all your touchpoints, all methods you use to interact with users, online and offline, all internal applications, brick-and-mortar stores, call centers, as well as points-of-sale. Finally, make sure your framework incorporates *future innovation* by writing down any new digital properties and touchpoints that are being planned or are currently in the works.

When we get to the outer circle of the framework, which represents your **customer**, you'll list all the different audiences you serve—meaning each of the distinct customer and user demographics that are targeted by your company's brands and divisions.

One caveat when it comes to this last piece of your framework: Remember to include any potential *business* audiences. This, of course, is only relevant to companies that have properties that solely target businesses (in contrast to consumers). But it's important because, as you'll soon see, you may want to bundle these separately. Even if the property with the business audience is located in the same country as another property—and is managed by the same entity—by definition it lacks a common audience and therefore shouldn't be clumped together.

BUNDLING

Now that you've laid out all your information in the framework, it's time to look at how you can *simplify*. By this we mean evaluating **which digital properties' identity can be bundled together.**

You'll have to dig into many different variables. Which of your brands have the most common audience? Does the organizational structure of your company allow for, say, a US-based property and a Canadian property to be bundled? Do the different privacy laws in the two countries allow for it?

These are just some of the factors you'll need to consider. For example, there is also the question of management: Is it possible for the IT team or security team managing this or that application to be allocated together?

If it sounds overwhelming, don't fret. It's not as bad as it seems. There's a clear and easy sequence you will follow, a list of priorities, starting with the most critical concerns:

- First, you must figure out the common or overlapping audiences (or target audiences). How many common audiences do you have between your distinct properties and brands? Remember that audiences can be common based on not only type but also location. Looking at your framework, you might see, for example, that you have two or three of these in common.
- Then, you must look at privacy regulations. Which of your brands fall under the same regulations? If you can support multiple privacy regulations through a single system, then you can certainly do that. But at some point, it's not going to be possible anymore and you'll need to separate them.
- Next, you focus on how your legal entity is structured...
- How the *company* is structured...

- And finally, how the responsible *team* is structured. How does this team function? For example, some companies have a global IT team and others have different IT teams in each country. There's no one right way. It all depends on how you want to deploy.

Which of your digital properties can be bundled together under one identity system?

APPLYING CIAM TO YOUR BUNDLES

To recap: At this point, based on all the different elements that came out of your framework, you have already looked closely at everything that could potentially be bundled. Now, it's time for you to apply the concept of CIAM to each bundle. **All the different properties within a bundle will share a single database and identity.**

As you can see in the following example, you have one cloud database at the center, and all the websites and third-party applications are connected to it. One user, one location, and one identity.

Now, for each bundle, you're going to need to do your implementation thinking and planning. That means figuring out your user migration, i.e., how you migrate existing users. For instance, if you bundle four websites together, all those users will have to be migrated into a single database.

You'll also need to figure out your privacy and security practices. How is your privacy statement going to be applied to the new bundle? This is a task that must be assigned to your legal team. They will have to study the new bundle and come up with a proposal. Same with the security team: They'll study the security and propose what the new security situation will have to look like.

What about user experience? How are you going to apply experience to the new bundle? This is something for the marketing team and product team to look into.

Finally, how are you going to apply infrastructure? This is obviously the functional responsibility of the engineering team.

Point is, by looking at all these pieces and making these decisions, you come to know exactly what solution is preferable for you.

But then you also need to figure out what sort of deployment you want, which means deciding **whether to go with a cloud solution or an on-premises solution.**

CLOUD VS. ON-PREMISES

How do you decide? It all depends on your organization and its business priorities.

We will dive into this question in depth in Chapter Fourteen. But for now, begin by asking yourself, *what kind of company are we?* When it comes to your computing, are you *already* largely cloud-based? If so, then you should almost certainly go with a cloud solution.

If not, you should still consider where you might be headed in the next five to ten years. Are you migrating toward the cloud? If so, you're probably better off adopting a cloud-based solution *now* so you don't need to migrate again later.

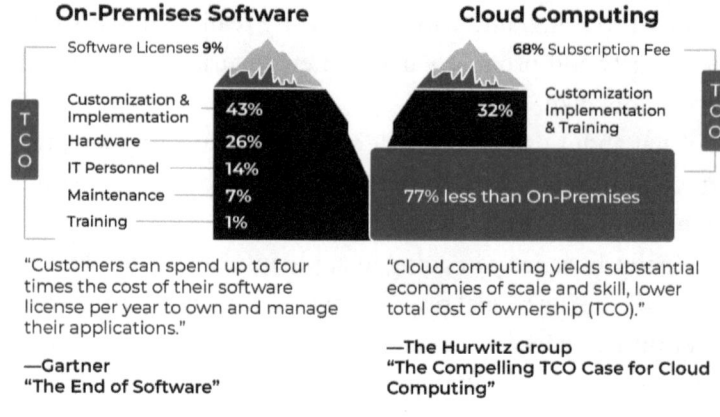

"Customers can spend up to four times the cost of their software license per year to own and manage their applications."

—Gartner
"The End of Software"

"Cloud computing yields substantial economies of scale and skill, lower total cost of ownership (TCO)."

—The Hurwitz Group
"The Compelling TCO Case for Cloud Computing"

In making this decision about cloud vs. on-premises, you should also think about where your users are located. If your audience is small and limited to a specific region, an on-premises solution might be okay. But **if you have a massive user base spread out over a hundred different countries, clearly an on-premises solution is not going to work!**

A cloud solution is possible in all cases, but an on-premises solution only works when the audience is small and localized.

Finally, if you do choose cloud, there is one more decision to be made, whether to go with a **public or private cloud** solution.

The reason this matters is that some companies prefer to manage their own data in their own environment versus leaving it with the vendors. For obvious reasons, banks, healthcare companies, and other organizations that store important personal data like to have full control of how they manage and secure everything.

What about you? Are you comfortable with a private cloud solution?

WHAT COMES NEXT

In summary, by this stage in your journey you've made a number of key decisions—decisions based on the unique circumstances within your organization. You've used what you learned to come up with a personalized strategy.

Now that you have your framework, how do you go about designing and developing your consumer identity *experience*?

CHAPTER TEN

CONSUMER IDENTITY EXPERIENCE: DESIGN AND DEVELOPMENT

Before we get into consumer *identity* experience—or IDx as we call it (ID for identity, x for experience)—we should be clear on what we mean by consumer experience in general. Gartner defines it as "the customer's perceptions and related feelings caused by the one-off and cumulative effects of their interactions with suppliers, employees, channels, and products."[20]

Notice how Gartner uses the words "perceptions" and "feelings." The consumer experience is *subjective*. But that doesn't mean it's not important. Quite the opposite. In fact, according to *PWC*, 73 percent of US consumers say that customer experience is an important factor in their buying

---

[20] "Customer Experience," Gartner, accessed June 25, 2024, https://www.gartner.com/en/information-technology/glossary/customer-experience.

decision.[21] But the same study shows that only 49 percent believe today's companies provide a good experience!

According to the same report, 43 percent of consumers are willing to *pay more* for a better experience.[22] All these findings speak to the same conclusion: customers place tremendous value on experience, and even if a company has a better product and/or better price than its competitors, clearly that doesn't mean it can afford to neglect the piece of the puzzle that is consumer experience.

It's not rocket science: When a company provides a great experience, customers tend to *like* them and want to continue to do business with them for a long time, as well as recommend them to others. Sure, having an amazing price or an amazing one-time product can help a company gain some wins initially—but keeping those customers and continuing to sell to them is always a much trickier proposition.

After all, consumers are under no obligation to stick with a company. If the experience is not good, they can just go somewhere else. It's the nature of business today: Customers will *always* be looking for an amazing experience, based on what they have seen with other beloved products or companies. If you can't provide that to them, they're out the door.

> There is a reason that Amazon has built a consumer-obsessed culture.

---

[21] Tom Puthiyamadam and José Reyes, *Experience Is Everything: Here's How to Get It Right* (PwC, 2018), 5, https://www.pwc.com/us/en/advisory-services/publications/consumer-intelligence-series/pwc-consumer-intelligence-series-customer-experience.pdf.

[22] Puthiyamadam and Reyes, *Experience Is Everything.*

So, that's consumer experience in a nutshell. But what about consumer *identity* experience or IDx?

The point we want to make here is that consumer identity experience is a critical piece of the broader consumer experience—and one that can have an outsized impact on businesses and their bottom lines.

THE FINANCIAL IMPACT OF CONSUMER IDENTITY EXPERIENCE

Why is IDx so important for businesses?

First, it's because **conversion metrics depend heavily on identity experience.** How many of the users who visit your website end up becoming your customer? Of course, we all want that percentage to be as high as possible. But a poor IDx can turn people off before you even have a chance to convert them.

What's more, we've seen that **the cost to acquire a user can be drastically reduced if you are able to provide a great consumer identity experience.**

Finally, a great IDx has been **shown to drastically increase customer retention and engagement.**

All you have to do is take a look at these three core metrics to see why customer identity experience has such a direct and profound impact on your revenue.

It all comes down to this: The identity experience is a make-or-break inflection point in the relationship with the consumer. If someone is struggling to log in or annoyed with the password reset process, they'll just call it quits.

But on a happier note, if you get this piece *right*, it can be your stepping stone in taking an unknown visitor and turning them into a real customer. Think of it like a blind date. This is stage one in your potential relationship. Don't mess up the first impression!

Of course, this advice doesn't apply in quite the same way to the identity experience of *employees* interacting with a company in a work capacity (a.k.a. IAM, which we talked about in Chapter Three). Although their IDx may also be glaringly subpar, usually they just suck it up and learn to deal—even if the processes they have to navigate are complicated and confusing—because they want to keep their jobs.

The difference lies in *control*. A consumer can leave a company at any time. They have control. But with employees, it's the company that holds the upper hand.

That doesn't mean that companies should ignore internal identity experience, but for the purposes of this book, we are focusing on how to design and develop a great *consumer* IDx.

UNDERSTANDING IDENTITY EXPERIENCE

Whether you're a CIO, CTO, or CDO, in thinking about your customer identity program, you need to focus on the overall flow. By that we mean how you define the strategy and development of your consumer identity experience altogether.

There are seven stages to this flow—**visitor experience, registration, password retrieval, login, pre-access, active access, and logout**—and they map closely to the seven components of CIAM architecture outlined in Chapter Nine.

Here, however, we are talking specifically about identity experience. These stages represent the typical user journey, from the time they come in as a visitor to when they log out and leave.

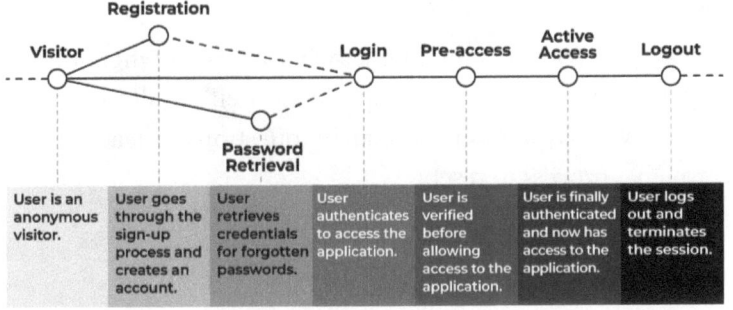

Let's look at the stages one by one.

VISITOR EXPERIENCE

When a user goes to, say, Amazon or Walmart.com, for the first time, they are just browsing, looking at the products and getting information as a visitor. They haven't yet registered or logged in.

This is the first stage for almost every application, not just e-commerce but government sites and more—and not just websites but all sorts of interfaces (mobile apps, smart TVs, IoT). Wherever a user goes, the first thing they do is browse, and only then do they register.

REGISTRATION

Registration happens when the user decides they like your product or services and want to do business with you. That's when they provide information like their name and email and create a password.

The registration process also includes verification via email or phone, welcome email, and profile creation on the backend.

PASSWORD RETRIEVAL

Password *retrieval* is, of course, what happens when a user forgets their password. The application either allows them to retrieve it by answering security questions or leads them through a process to reset.

LOGIN OR AUTHENTICATE

When a user registers with an application—back in the second stage of this process—they have to verify their email and, in some cases, other pertinent information like their phone number or driver's license. Different applications require different kinds of verification.

But *after* they've been verified, they can just log in because now they have the credentials to do so.

PRE-ACCESS

Once a user logs into an application, what happens in the backend is that the app runs through a bunch of different access levels for that person: whether they are authorized to log in, whether they might be a fraudulent user, whether they have certain kinds of verification already in play. The app also checks whether the user has accepted the privacy policy or not.

This all falls under the category of *pre-access*, an internal process that happens in a fraction of a second every time someone tries to log in. Even though the user is technically already logged in, the system is still busy performing various actions in the backend, such as checking the person's credit and making sure it's not a fraud account or a hacker.

ACTIVE ACCESS

During that moment of pre-access described above, some of the capabilities and features of the application are unavailable. But once everything has been verified, the user is moved to what's called *active access*. Their authenticating credentials have been confirmed. The application knows their location and whether they are a full user or not. They know that the user is legitimate and not a bot.

Moreover, once the system has granted active access, the user has free rein of all the operations available to them. If it's an e-commerce site, they can now make purchases. They can do things like editing their credit card information or updating their history or preferences.

LOGOUT

Finally, of course, when the user is done with whatever their purpose was for visiting a particular application, they log out—and all the sessions and credentials are purged from the backend.

> The seven stages of consumer IDx are visitor experience, registration, password retrieval, login, pre-access, active access, and logout.

These seven stages are the inflection points you need to think about when building the consumer IDx within your own company. Keep in mind that users can *and do* drop out of the funnel at any one of these thresholds.

For example, you may have a million visitors but half of them leave before attempting to register. Out of the remaining

500,000, maybe only 300,000 actually succeed in signing up. That can happen easily if the email verification process is confusing or the verification email winds up in users' spam filter.

Generally, there is a drop-off at each one of the seven stages. At each inflection point, the consumer is confronted with a decision: Do they want to continue their relationship with your brand or not? That is why it is so important to understand this flow and get it right.

So, how then should you go about designing and developing a phenomenal identity experience for your consumers—one that grows your business rather than strains it?

DESIGNING AND DEVELOPING IDENTITY EXPERIENCE

First, you have to *prepare*. That means conducting initial research, discussing, and brainstorming. Specifically, it means creating and defining your **consumer persona**. Who are your customers? If, for example, they're fifteen to twenty-two years old (which is the case with a company like Snapchat), obviously you should plan on designing the experience differently than you would if you were, say, a healthcare provider.

Don't take shortcuts when it comes to this crucial step of defining your consumer persona. You need to really do the research and probably include not just one but a few (up to five) different personas. Not every company has a single consumer persona. For many businesses, the customer base is made up of multiple categories of people who will be going through the IDx.

Take the time to learn about your customers and understand their psyches, emotions, and needs. What are each of them expecting from the identity experience and what struggles or challenges might they encounter?

Now, it's time to map your users' journeys using a concept called **empathy mapping**. To understand the needs of your customers, you need to show empathy toward them, know what they're looking for and what pain point you're trying to solve for them.

TASKS
What tasks are users trying to complete? What questions do they need answered?

FEELINGS
How is the user feeling about the experience? What really matters to them?

INFLUENCES
What people, things, or places may influence how the user acts?

PAIN POINTS
What pain points might the user be experiencing that they hope to overcome?

OVERALL GOAL
What is the user's ultimate goal? What are they trying to achieve?

By combining your consumer personas with your empathy mapping, you are trying to get as complete a picture as possible of your customers—and what actions they might take as a result of their beliefs and emotions.

Next comes something called **stakeholder mapping**. Of course, a company's IDx cannot just be designed based on the research and input of one person—say, a marketing manager—within a company. It requires participation and buy-in from all the stakeholders: the marketing team, product team, security team, customer success team, and more. All parties need to be brought together in alignment and collaboration.

To make this happen, first, you must identify who the various stakeholders are and what their needs and interests might be. What are the potential risks they see? What are the three or four challenges they want to solve through the IDx?

Once you've succeeded in aligning stakeholder intent, you should now be ready to focus on actually *designing* the experience by mapping it all out—based on the core challenges and objectives identified by the various stakeholders.

In mapping the identity experience journey, make sure to customize it to your business. Maybe you only have a website. Or maybe you have a website and a mobile app. **It is important to map your IDx specifically to your brand, as well as your business platforms, technologies, subsidiaries, and anything else that is unique to you.**

Finally, *developing* the experience means using all this knowledge and research and applying it to each inflection point—figuring out how to best track user browsing, how to host the login and registration pages to make them as fast and easy to use as possible, and how to deliver high performance throughout.

When it comes to registration, for example, does the user receive a verification email in a matter of seconds or minutes?

There are so many tools you can use to develop and so many ways to improve your identity experience, but again the elements you use will depend on factors that are unique to each organization. On which platforms are your consumers interacting? Web? Web and mobile? Smart TV? IoT?

Last but not least, of course, you must pass everything you've now mapped over to your engineering group to *develop* the experience for you.

CHAPTER ELEVEN

CIAM SECURITY AND PRIVACY: DESIGN AND DEVELOPMENT

When developing the CIAM strategy for your company, regulatory and security considerations *must* be front of mind. How will your customer-facing identity solution stay compliant with government regulations? How will it meet security requirements?

Getting this part right means meeting regularly with your security team to answer such questions. That's important because, again, CIAM is not something you can execute and implement just on your own. It's an organization-level initiative, not specific to engineering or marketing or any one division. But sometimes one of these teams will try to push their own goals, and that can create an internal tug-of-war. You might hear statements like, *if we do such-and-such, we can get more users and more revenue,* and feel pressure to cut corners with security and privacy.

Or you may find that security and privacy considerations just wind up at the bottom of the totem pole because people don't understand all the elements involved, which somehow renders the concerns a low priority. But make no mistake: This kind of indifference poses a huge risk to businesses.

Just ask the hotel chain Marriott. A security breach exposed the data of 500 million Marriott customers, and they had to pay around $23.8 million in penalties under the GDPR's privacy regulations.[23] Did they deliberately turn a blind eye to vulnerabilities in their system? Probably not. But clearly, they did not prioritize security and privacy considerations—and so they had to suffer the consequences.

This happens all the time, and not only to the huge companies you hear about like Google and Facebook (both of which the EU has put massive penalties on), but also smaller enterprises. It may not make the news, but these events are just as painful, if not more.

And the damage goes beyond dollars and cents. When you take your eye off the ball of security and privacy, it's not just your customer data that is at risk of being breached. It's also their trust. Mess this up and they won't want to do business with you.

Fines and penalties are one thing, but damage to your brand's reputation and loss of your existing customer base can often be the kiss of death.

---

23 Natasha Lomas, "UK Watchdog Reduces Marriott Data Breach Fine to $23.8M, Down from $123M," TechCrunch, October 30, 2020, https://techcrunch.com/2020/10/30/uk-watchdog-reduces-marriott-data-breach-fine-to-23-8m-down-from-123m/.

REGULATORY AND SECURITY CONSIDERATIONS GO HAND IN HAND

When we talk about *regulatory* considerations, we mean actions that are required by local or federal governments in the region where you're operating your business. For example, the US requires that liquor content not be pushed to users under twenty-one. And the EU requires that all businesses store consumer data within EU territory.

On one level, these requirements may not seem *fundamental* to your business in the same way as other core concerns like growing your customer base or ROI. But if you break them and have to suffer the legal and financial consequences, well, trust us when we say you'll wish you had taken them more seriously.

What about *security* considerations? How are those different from *privacy* concerns?

The short answer is this: With security, it's not about a government requiring you to protect your consumers, but how much your brand's reputation depends on it. Whereas privacy is specifically focused on protecting users' PII, security is a broader initiative to protect users' data and accounts.

Nonetheless, the two are very related, and the distinction is often irrelevant in practice. If security is breached, by definition it means personal information is breached—in violation of privacy regulations. And that means you can expect penalties.

Yes, there are examples of privacy incidents that don't involve security breaches. For example, maybe a company gets in trouble for sending their customers lots of emails without consent. In that case, the issue wouldn't be that personal information was breached but that the consumer's right to privacy was broken.

But when a security breach happens, like with Marriott, automatically it's considered a breach of regulatory compliance as well—meaning that the government is probably going to get involved. That's because regulations require that you protect your customers' data and follow certain processes to do so. If security is breached, it's because you've failed to follow those regulations and government standards.

To put it succinctly: **Security and government regulations around privacy are not really two separate things. If the former is breached, the latter is too.**

But for the purpose of this chapter, we are breaking them up so that we can look in depth at how you should be incorporating both security and regulatory considerations into your CIAM strategy.

YOUR SECURITY STRATEGY

What are the best practices you need to follow strictly from a security angle? What do you need to consider in terms of protecting your customers' data from being breached by a cyber-attack?

Most brands, understandably, place customer experience, generating ROI, and growing the company at the top of their business agenda. But in order to ensure nothing gets in the way of those goals, you need to understand security. You can't risk security in a bid to optimize other business matters.

> Security is an essential element of your business and must never be compromised. Nor should it be left alone or ignored.

Part of the process, when designing and developing your security strategy, is to assess the inherent risk that comes with your particular application. Some are at a much higher risk than others. For example, a news site is low risk: Chances are the only personal information it stores are the email addresses of its readers. But other applications like e-commerce sites are high-risk: They handle and store sensitive data like credit card information. And a banking or financial site poses an even higher risk.

Healthcare applications and health insurance providers are also commonly thought of as high-risk because they hold sensitive, confidential information about patients.

What about you? You must assess the risk of your own applications by looking at what kind of consumer information you deal with. Then, based on that, consider the security of your application.

You must also distinguish between the security protections necessary for your customers versus your employees. They are different. Not because one group's security is more important than the other, but because there is more risk among the consumer-facing applications. Employees are in the office, or at least accessing the application on known laptops and devices, whereas customers are using the customer-facing application from all over, on every kind of device, at every touchpoint. The security implications are not comparable: On the consumer side, it's both higher volume and higher risk. They also have separate security technologies and practices.

But once you assess the risk on both the consumer and employee side, you have to think about what kind of security strategy you're going to pursue. What kind of **password** policies are you going to use? How complex will you require your customers' passwords to be? What will the expiration time be for the passwords? How will you secure them for your customers? What kind of encryption will you use?

Because the customer-facing application exists on the internet, you have to make sure it's protected from brute-force attacks and dictionary attacks. What's the difference between the two? The former is what happens when somebody in the cyber world creates a bot or machine that can identify usernames and passwords. It does this by running through millions of options at incredible speed. The latter uses the dictionary to identify potential password combinations and ultimately the password of the account-holder.

Both are common in the industry. Luckily, there are controls that companies can use on their online applications to protect against them.

> What kind of controls do you have in place to protect against brute-force and dictionary cyber-attacks?

Then, you also have to think about your **step-up authentication**. When your users log in, there should be an additional layer of authentication required to connect to your application. That way, even if one layer is breached, the second will protect the accounts.

Second-factor authentication, for example, is a form of step-up authentication where the customer is asked a question or sent a code to verify using SMS, email, or, often these days, a Google authenticator. It is an important extra layer of security and one that can largely be automated. This is true of most security controls nowadays.

Technology has come a long way. Just as cybercriminals have gotten more advanced, so has the tech.

Because of these advances in technology, businesses can automatically detect many risks they couldn't in the past. They can identify a user's location, behavior, and how the person is using their application compared to how they did previously. There are all kinds of intelligent ways in which companies can now identify whether it's really the same person as the digital identity being used.

Then, in addition to two-factor authentication, companies are now using something called **environment security**, which means what wherever the application is hosted (on the company's own servers or a cloud provider), they know what security controls are in place to protect not just the individual user but the whole environment, including the server and database.

> "Environment security" allows companies to know what kind of encryption or cryptographic keys are being used to secure the whole environment of their server and database, who has access, what the firewalls are, and what controls are in place.

YOUR STRATEGY FOR REGULATION COMPLIANCE

Government regulations keep evolving, and there have been some big new ones—such as the GDPR, the CCPA, and BIP EBA—that have made noise in recent years.

There are also many industry-specific regulations, such as the Health Insurance Portability and Accountability Act (HIPAA), which requires healthcare organizations to:

- Ensure appropriate safeguards to protect the privacy of personal health information.
- Set limits and conditions on the uses and disclosures that may be made of such information without patient authorization.
- Give patients various rights over their own health information, such as the right to examine and obtain a copy of their health records and request corrections.

But the explosion of regulations we've seen in recent years runs the gamut across different industries—and also of course there are many that apply more broadly, like the Payment Card Industry Data Security Standard (PCI DSS) that must be adopted by *any* organization, in any business arena, that collects debit and credit card information. This law requires companies to formulate policies to protect their consumers' information and ensure that they manage and store card data without any loopholes. It even extends to organizations that process card payments using third-party vendors.

To reiterate: This wave of regulation isn't something that's just happening in the US or Canada or the EU; in today's world, new ones are popping up in virtually *every* nation.

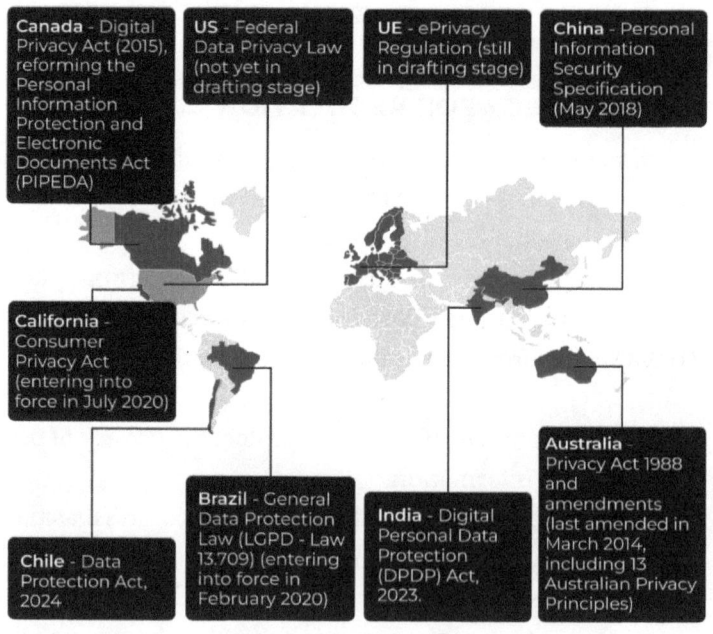

While there are some differences between these laws, largely having to do with location, overall, they're remarkably similar. The key objective is securing customer data, giving customers more control over their personal information and preventing breaches. When data breaches do happen, governments impose hefty penalties. But the idea behind the laws is that the threat of penalty will get companies to take privacy seriously and maintain strong controls.

Some of the government regulations focus on customer data *collection,* i.e., what kinds of data companies should be allowed to collect and what kinds are off limits. This has the effect of making sure companies are always careful about what information they are asking for from their consumers.

In a bigger sense, **the goal of these regulations around data collection is to give back *control* to the consumer.** What do we mean by control? At any time, consumers should be able to delete their account, delete their information, and change or update their information. The consumer always has the *right of access*, meaning they can access their own personal information—as well as change, update, or remove it—whenever they want.

Not only that, but the consumer has to *consent* to any communication from the company, and this consent needs to be formally captured to show that the consumer has indeed allowed it.

Finally, regulation compliance means that, in protecting the privacy of their consumers' data, companies may not share it with any third party. They have to make sure the data has not been breached and *cannot* be breached.

Of course, with some applications, their very business model is based on sharing third-party data, but regulations dictate that the sharing be transparent. They have to ask the consumer for permission beforehand.

> Your strategy for regulatory compliance must encompass data collection, consent, and privacy.

Given the slew of new regulations around consumer data, it has become all the more important—in creating your CIAM strategy—to have a single holistic, centralized view of your consumer, something that both you and they can see.

You need to be able to easily look and know exactly where the data is located, who it is shared with (which third parties, if any), and what kind of consent has been provided.

The *location of data* is especially relevant these days because a lot of governments now require that data be stored in the same region where a company is based. Today's companies have to think about not just whether their consumer-facing process is compliant with regulations, but also the internal environment where they host and store the data.

Making matters even more complicated, if a US company, for example, has consumers based in other parts of the world, it has to make sure it's complying with government regulations for all the different regions where it has customers. If there are users in Australia, for instance, their data needs to be stored in Australia.

CHAPTER TWELVE

FLOW OF DIGITAL ID IN YOUR ECOSYSTEM

In Chapters Ten and Eleven, you learned how to design and develop your consumer experience strategy and your security and privacy strategy. At the heart of it all, of course, is *data*. Sensitive consumer data is *why* security hygiene has become so important. At a fundamental level, it's why you have come to this book: to learn about a centralized identity management strategy that will funnel all your customer PII sources into a single data repository.

In this chapter, we will show you the nuts and bolts of *data integration* (DI) within your business and ecosystem.

Data integration is what allows for the flow of digital identity into a single view. The consumer sends a request for data to a master server. The server collects the necessary data from both internal and external sources. And crucially, the data is unified in a coherent form and addressed to the consumer after extraction.

That's when the actual analysis begins—and data integration comes into play.

WHY DATA INTEGRATION IS SO IMPORTANT

Data integration saves time on the processing of data and the value extraction from it. Instead of having to create ties between distinct subsystems, employees can access the entire system.

Imagine a brand struggling to identify its customers accurately; it's like trying to solve a puzzle with missing pieces! This skews the analytics and makes it tough to really understand what customers want and how they behave across different digital platforms.

Think about it: Brands gather customer data from all over—websites, mobile apps, marketing tools, e-commerce sites, and customer service systems—hoping to piece together insights that enhance the customer experience.

But often, these data sources end up in silos, creating a jumbled view of customers. This not only hampers effective analysis but also makes it hard to personalize the experience.

Imagine walking into a store where the staff knows you only from one visit; they will likely miss your preferences! That's what happens when customer data isn't integrated.

On the flip side, the benefits of data integration allow you to:

- **Connect Disparate Systems:** CIAM seamlessly consolidates user identities across various data systems into one unified platform, ensuring a single source of truth.
- **Link Data Effortlessly:** Information from different systems—like CRM, Customer Service, and Billing—becomes interconnected, all tied to those unified customer identities within CIAM.
- **Reduce Redundancy:** By eliminating the need to maintain separate customer identities across enterprise systems, you significantly minimize the chances of data duplication.
- **Enhance Data Integrity:** This leads to better data integrity, making it easier to trust the information at your fingertips.

- **Streamline Customer Data Management:** Ultimately, it establishes a cohesive approach to customer data management, allowing for smarter decision-making and improved customer experiences.

All in all, by allowing various applications to easily feed customer information to and from the CIAM data repository, data integration gives you a comprehensive picture of each of your customers and enables leveraging data in various marketing and business applications. Reporting becomes that much smoother. And it's now that much easier to keep all your procedures up to date.

> Data integration saves time on the processing of data and extracting value from it—by making it accessible.

YOUR OPTIONS FOR DATA INTEGRATION APPROACHES

There is no one-size-fits-all approach to data integration, but all solutions have certain components in common, such as a data source network or a master server. DI has evolved so much over the past decade that there are now many wonderful options.

Initially, there was only one technology for batch data integration, and that was ETL (extract, transform, load). But as organizations began to incorporate more outlets into their data ecosystem, they started to require *real-time* data integration—and so, new innovations were implemented to meet these needs.

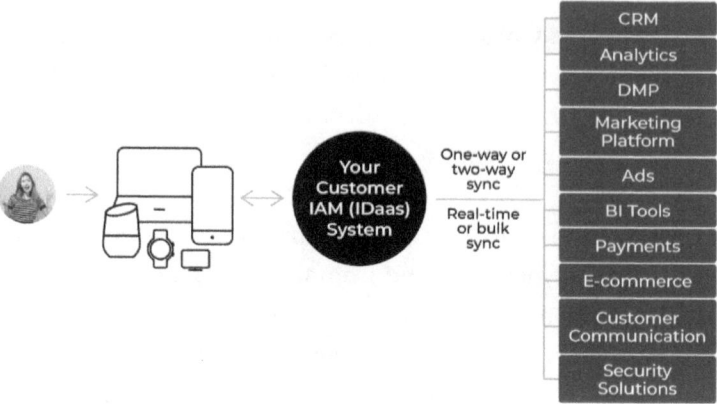

Nowadays, when it comes to approaches to data integration, companies have an array of choices, including:

- **Data Consolidation.** This involves physically bringing together data from several different systems into one consolidated data store. (ETL supports data consolidation.)
- **Data Propagation.** Here, you use applications to copy data from one location to another. (EAI and EDR technologies support data propagation.)
- **Data Virtualization.** When an interface is used to provide a nearly real-time, unified view of data from disparate sources with different data models, it means data can be *viewed* in one location but not *stored* in that single location.
- **Data Federation.** Technically a form of data virtualization, the federation approach uses a virtual database to create a common data model for assorted data from different systems. (EII is a technology that supports data federation.)

Those last two, data federation and data virtualization, are good workarounds for situations where data consolidation is cost-prohibitive or would cause too many security and compliance issues.

RISKS AND BEST PRACTICES FOR DATA INTEGRATION

Consumer data integration is defined as the process of synchronizing data about any website visitor, lead, or consumer that has ever interacted with your brand or product. It is about letting your team, tools, and data work together smoothly.

Toward that end, we want to share with you a few best practices for avoiding common pitfalls when integrating consumer data. When large amounts of data are transformed, organized, cleaned, and grouped into a single structure—as they are during data integration—there is the potential that these modifications could lead to a risk of data theft.

The following chart from DZone.com offers a helpful rundown of the most common such risks, as well as the solutions.

POTENTIAL PROJECT RISKS	BEST PRACTICE RECOMMENDATIONS
Uncertain Source Data Quality Data integration effort may not meet the planned schedule because the quality of source data is unknown or inadequate.	• Conduct formal data profiling of source data early (i.e., during requirements gathering) to understand whether data quality meets project needs. Inaccuracies, omissions, cleanliness, duplicates, and inconsistencies in the source data can be identified and resolved before or even during the extract/transform process. • Since duplicate data often exist in multiple source systems, identify all sources and discuss with the users which are most applicable. • Implement commercial/automated data quality tools accompanied by consultation and training.
Data Dictionaries and Data Models Are Flawed Data within sources and targets cannot be easily interpreted by developers and QA.	• Ensure accurate and current documentation of data models and mapping documents. • Use automated documentation tools. • Create meaningful documentation of data definitions and data descriptions in a data dictionary. • Create procedures for maintaining documentation in accordance with changes to the source systems. • Provide training to the QA team by data stewards/owners.

POTENTIAL PROJECT RISKS	BEST PRACTICE RECOMMENDATIONS
Source and Target Data Mapping Issues Source data may be inaccurately mapped due to the absence of data dictionaries and data models.	• Data dictionaries and data catalogs should be maintained to support all data associated with the project. Higher quality data mapping documents will be the result. • Implement a data mapping change control system to keep a record of every change.
Excessive Defects in Data Sources Data defects are found at a late stage during development.	• Ensure that data requirements are complete and that data dictionaries are available and current. • Profile all data sources and target data after each ETL. • Prepare to cleanse and fix dirty data. • Assure the continued maintenance of data mapping and all other specification documents.
No Master Test Plan (MTP) or Test Strategy Established A master test plan/strategy does not exist or is inadequate in scope.	• A *Test Strategy/Master Test Plan* documents the overall structure and objectives of all project testing—from unit testing to component to system and performance tests. The MTP covers activities over the data integration lifecycle and identifies evaluation criteria for the testers.

POTENTIAL PROJECT RISKS	BEST PRACTICE RECOMMENDATIONS
Excessive Defects in Target Data Much of the loaded target data is in error after ETL.	• Ensure that the target data sampling process is high quality. • Use test tools that provide extensive data coverage. • Choose a data sampling approach that's extensive enough to avoid missing defects in both source and target data. • Choose an appropriate technology to compare source and target data to determine whether both source and target are equal or target data has been transformed. • Verify that no data or metadata has been lost during ETL processes. The data warehouse must load all relevant data from the source application into the target according to business rules. • Check the correctness of surrogate keys that uniquely identify rows of data. • Check data loading status and error messages after ETL. • Verify that data types and formats are as specified during database design. • Verify that every ETL session is completed with only planned exceptions.
Project-Wide Testing Not Coordinated Inadequate or nonexistent source to target data flows tests.	• A data quality audit should include validation that the information in a source system (such as a CSV) is accurate so that there is a high level of confidence that it can be trusted when it is added to target integration.

POTENTIAL PROJECT RISKS	BEST PRACTICE RECOMMENDATIONS
Staff Testing Skills Are Insufficient Qualified resources with the required knowledge of data integration testing are unavailable.	• Invest in data integration testing courses and training resources, recruit staff with data testing experience, and engage services consultants. • Invest in specialized data roles: data analysts, data quality analysts, data testing toolset skills, and data engineers.
Source to Target Data Transformation Code Is Complex Complex transformations without required test tools or tester skills may not be easy to test.	• Early validation of table join complexity, queries, and resulting business reports. • Clarify business requirements; develop and test pseudo queries before programming data extractions and loads. • Validate the number and accessibility of source data fields.
Planned Testing Is Predominantly Manual Minimal testing automation has been adopted for ETL, data profiling, unit, and regression tests.	• Invest in automated unit and regression test tools for faster and reusable testing suites. • Consider automation testing tools available for metadata verifications, data format checking, row counts, uniqueness checks, data cleansing, load tests, performance tests, and smoke tests.
Data Volume Scalability Causes Performance Issues Growing data volumes due to changing requirements.	• Employ skills and toolsets for data volume estimations. • Load the database with the peak expected production volumes to help ensure that the amount of data can be loaded by the ETL process within the agreed-on time window.

WHAT COMES NEXT

A well-designed enterprise data integration tool empowers organizations to break down data silos and create a unified data set that's accessible to all. It helps you accomplish your business goals and make the most of the latest technologies in your company.

Given all these advantages, it's no wonder so many companies that handle sensitive data are turning to CIAM. Centralized identity is one of the most effective systems for managing and maintaining a strong security posture. In the following chapter, we will take a deep dive into all the essential capabilities of your CIAM solution.

CHAPTER THIRTEEN

CIAM ESSENTIAL CAPABILITIES

At this point in the book, you now have a good understanding of what digital identity *is*: namely, a set of properties about a consumer that can be conveniently calculated and documented digitally. You are also well aware of how CIAM works to enable real-time identity management, end-to-end security, and activation—while creating seamless and scalable digital experiences for your consumers.

Your consumers are, of course, the ones responsible for helping generate revenue for your business—and not only does CIAM help boost your intelligence around this valuable group, but it also allows you to better *cross-market* to them (by facilitating data sharing among your systems and applications).

A strong CIAM solution will also support such features as modern authentication, social logins, account verification, SSO, MFA, adaptive authentication, directory service storage, data processing and maintenance, zero trust security, and user management.

Furthermore, **CIAM solutions work just as well with other categories of users** (i.e., not just consumers), including contractors, partners, and all outside stakeholders or members of the value chain.

With consumers and external shareholders alike, CIAM allows for secure, low-friction access to numerous engagement channels, such as the web and mobile. And for businesses like yours that choose to implement a CIAM solution, the benefits are wide-ranging. They include:

- Seamless authentication to different consumer-facing properties,
- Massive scalability (by virtue of being able to anticipate surges and dips in consumer activity),
- Unified consumer experience across all touchpoints,
- Constant protection of consumer data and accounts,
- Adherence to privacy regulations for protecting data (in transit and at rest), and
- Ability to connect all native and third-party applications that handle consumer data, such as seamless integration with CRM.

In this chapter, we will dive into all the major components of digital identity and your CIAM solution.

MODERN REGISTRATION AND AUTHENTICATION

First, when it comes to identifying new prospects, the most important threshold is **registration**. Here you are asking your potential consumer to share details about themselves for the first time. How do you streamline this experience and ensure that the process is seamless across all applications?

First, you have to enable convenient registration features like social registration and passwordless login. You also need to provide customized registration forms that genuinely reflect your brand.

> Give your consumers a full suite of self-service tools, and not only will you deliver to them a safer and more convenient experience, but you'll see significantly more conversions—and less abandonment!

Then, once you've registered your new customer, you move on to **authentication**. Remember, people don't want to have to enter a new set of credentials for every application. They expect to be able to access *what they want when they want it.*

CIAM makes this possible by providing a centralized authentication mechanism across all your applications and comes with out-of-the-box authentication methods like standard username/password login, social login, phone login, and passwordless login.

SINGLE SIGN-ON AND FEDERATION

SSO is one of the biggest factors in how CIAM works to improve the overall consumer experience. It allows users to log into multiple independent applications—including third-party apps, apps in the cloud, and any related (yet independent) software/platform inside your organization—with a single set of credentials (single ID and password). Moreover, rather than having to re-enter these credentials to access different services, they only enter their login *once.*

Through this process of authentication, instead of having to waste time and energy logging into different applications separately, customers are empowered to obtain quick access to *all* applications. This is made possible through **web SSO** (which allows consumers to access any connected web properties with a single identity), **mobile SSO** (which does the same except it unifies sessions across multiple connected mobile applications), and **federated SSO** (which utilizes Identity Providers (IDPs) to store and authenticate identities to log into third-party web portals, mobile apps, and more).

With that last one, federated SSO, several identity protocols (including SAML, JWT, OpenID Connect, OAuth, and Multipass) can be used to authenticate consumers. And as you know from the previous chapter about data integration, the *federation* approach to identity flow—which uses a virtual database to create a common model for assorted data from different systems—can be beneficial in circumstances where consolidation is cost-prohibitive or would create too many headaches around security and compliance. Federated SSO, therefore, works just like SSO but within other organizations and is established when multiple brands work together with trust, sharing resources to authorize and authenticate one another's customers.

These days, many organizations are doing just that: developing identity federations where many users can access many resources using a single login and authentication system. In fact, the demand for federated SSO keeps on growing as enterprises look to step out ahead of the curve to deliver a zero-friction experience to their consumers.

SELF-SERVICE CONSUMER EXPERIENCE

According to Zendesk, 67 percent of consumers prefer self-service over speaking to a company representative.[24] When interacting with your applications, they don't want to get assistance from a customer service agent (CSA). They want to be self-sufficient. But that only works if your brand's self-service capabilities are well-planned and executed.

To deliver what your customers want—fast, flexible support that allows them to solve their *own* problems, at their convenience, on their own schedule—you need to focus on creating smart and efficient strategies in the following key areas:

- **Passwordless login.** This simplifies and streamlines the authentication process by swapping traditional passwords with more secure methods like email-based login, SMS-based login, social login, and fingerprints.
- **Password reset.** This gives consumers a safe, seamless self-service backup for when they forget their passwords (or have them stolen).
- **Profile management.** This puts consumers in the driver's seat by allowing them to control and manage their own account details, such as their preferences for messages, offers, and services.
- **Add/delete account.** This allows consumers to make their own decisions about adding new users or deleting accounts.
- **Consent and preference management.** Finally, this feature lets consumers manage their own consent and preferences.

---

[24] "Self-Service: Do Customers Want to Help Themselves?" *Zendesk Blog*, last updated May 17, 2023, https://www.zendesk.com/blog/searching-for-self-service/.

MULTI FACTOR AUTHENTICATION

With MFA, new layers of security are added to the authentication process, usually in the form of numeric or alphanumeric codes. These extra layers—which use SMS, email, or push notifications—can be either compulsory or optional. But the idea is that adding the step (or steps) to verify identities helps ensure that the right consumer has the right access to your network. It takes the burden (of stolen or lost passwords) off consumers and makes it harder for bad actors to get into their accounts.

Password — Second Factor — Access

With **SMS-based authentication,** the account provider sends the consumer a text message containing an OTP in addition to the traditional username and password verification. With **email-based authentication,** the consumer is sent the OTP via email—and this can also work as a backup method if a mobile device is lost or stolen.

Other forms of multifactor authentication include security questions, biometric verification, automated phone calls, Google Authenticator, and social login.

ADAPTIVE AUTHENTICATION

Adaptive authentication, also known as risk-based authentication, is an advanced method that uses real-time intelligence to determine risk on a consumer account and take appropriate action, such as triggering a two-factor authentication to protect the user's account. It works by analyzing risk scores based on contextual factors like:

1. What is the registered login device, browser, and device OS (operating system)?
2. Is the information entered (about the consumer's identity) the same as what's stored in the directory?
3. Did the login come from a suspicious or unknown "geolocation"?
4. What is the location and time of the suspicious login compared to the last login attempt? (This is known as "geo-velocity.")
5. What are the personal characteristics of the user (e.g., job roles or history of security incidents)?
6. How many failed login attempts have there been?

Based on where the consumer lands with each of these factors, they can either gain access to their accounts directly using familiar modes of authentication (like a password) or provide additional verification (security questions, OTP, biometrics, PIN, etc.) to gain access.

DATA STORAGE AND DIRECTORY SERVICE

A good CIAM solution allows you to flexibly build schemas to make the most of your consumer profile storage. Traditionally, organizations have stored all their consumer identities within one single silo. But now, by using multiple repositories, you can benefit from such advantages as:

- increased responsiveness (because, with separate identity stores, connecting applications have fewer entries to search),
- security-based segregation (between enterprise and non-enterprise identities, which no longer run the risk of getting mixed together because they are now separated into two directory services, with enterprise directories as the front-line gateway to the network), and
- better organization of data (services now only need to be as broad or deep as required for their use cases, which means directories are easier to navigate and administer, and you can also have a more streamlined directory information tree [DIT]).

It is critical to have a directory solution tailored to build rich consumer profiles, but of course all that data has to also be safely secured. Security teams need to understand how data is stored for various use cases and then need to follow best practices around *controls* (physical, technical, and administrative/compliance).

Using secure identity and access controls to process and maintain consumer data is what your CIAM solution is all about. But **scalability and performance** are key. No matter the size of your business and whether you're dealing with thousands of digital profiles or hundreds of millions, your solution should deliver instant, frictionless access during unexpected traffic spikes and as your consumer base grows.

It's worth mentioning here that, when it comes to data processing, a multi-tenant cloud model works best for use cases where registration abandonment and revenue are at an all-time high. The multi-tenant cloud model is also good for system *maintenance*: Vulnerability fixes can be deployed in real time without service disruption.

Whether in the cloud or on premises, your CIAM solution requires **automatic backup and disaster recovery**. This is essential to keeping your business up and running without interruption.

Some choose, for example, to maintain their own data center and then use the cloud only for storage of backup or duplicate data. With this hybrid approach, they can still enjoy robust scalability without having to move their production environment.

Others, however, choose to use the cloud to host both their production and disaster-recovery centers.

ZERO TRUST SECURITY

Another approach to network security is to always be 100 percent strict about verifying identities—whether the consumer is located inside or outside the network perimeter. With zero trust security, the default stance is that no one is trusted.

This approach is only effective, however, when organizations track and verify the access rights and privileges of consumers on an ongoing basis. In order to enable zero trust security in a way that is both comprehensive and achievable, you have to make sure to:

- **Identify your protected surface.** Shift your focus from the "attack surface" to just your "protected surface," i.e., your data, applications, assets, and services (DAAS).
- **Map and architect your zero trust IT network.** Once you have successfully identified your protected surface, your next step is to document how the resources interact. Later, you can map out the best-fitting zero trust architecture for each use case.

- **Continuously monitor using zero trust security policies.** Once the network is built, you need to always be aware of who your consumers are, what applications they want to access and why, how they intend to connect, and how you can secure that access. Make sure to check authorization and authentication at every access request.

In creating a zero trust model, above all you have to keep in mind its capabilities for **adaptive authentication** and **multifactor authentication**. As for the former, the idea of course is to always be sure that your consumers are exactly who you think they are.

Adaptive authentication is based on a centrally managed authentication system, which keeps an eye on changes in behavior or context for all resources.

As for the second essential aspect of zero trust security, using multifactor authentication within your zero trust model will ensure that hackers cannot brute force their way into your network. MFA makes this possible, of course, by mandating at least two factors of verification (these can include SMS code, security questions, hard tokens, and more).

With zero trust security, *anyone* who wants to gain access to network resources—whether they're inside or outside the network perimeter—must first be authenticated.

COMPLIANCE WITH PRIVACY REGULATIONS

With all the new laws relating to PII cropping up around the world, it can be hard to keep track of all the different regulations and requirements.

The major ones that you need to be aware of have to do with the following:

- **Types of privacy data.** These laws deal with all categories of identity information, everything from name and address to political opinions and sexual orientation.
- **The right to access.** This allows consumers to access, review, and edit their data, as well as ask for additional information about the usage and disclosure of their data.
- **The right to object.** This allows consumers to object, stop, or prevent the use of their data for certain processes like direct marketing or statistical analysis.
- **The right to be forgotten.** This allows consumers to erase or delete their personal data, as well as restrict their exposure to third-party processing.
- **Consent.** These laws require companies to gather consent from consumers before collecting and processing personal data (consent that can also be withdrawn at any time).
- **Data portability.** These laws allow consumers to ask for copies of their data (in a commonly used, machine-readable format) and to transfer their data to other organizations.
- **Data security.** These laws require companies to implement appropriate security safeguards—such as encryption—to prevent consumer data from being wrongfully accessed, destroyed, modified, lost, or disclosed.

INTEGRATION WITH APIS

APIs (application programming interfaces) allow you to quickly integrate with third-party applications for functions like identity and marketing analytics, security integration, and provisioning/deprovisioning. APIs also allow organizations to *customize* the implementation, all the way down to the look and feel of the user interface. In particular, many companies use APIs to customize the so-called "last mile" of the user experience.

With your new CIAM solution, you'll be able to support integration with system types ranging from data stores and directory services to CRM and CMS, from data management and e-commerce platforms to marketing solutions and fraud detection engines.

Great third-party integration is key to unleashing the true potential of consumer data. It allows your business to connect to any software, device, or application—and harness these tools toward better marketing strategies, increased sales, and greater insights around consumer behavior. And of course, it saves you time and money that would otherwise be squandered building your own integrations.

In CIAM, you get crucial information *in real time* about your consumers and potential consumers. But you still need to be able to pull data and process it in a third-party application for more advanced analytics. You still need to integrate marketing tools that can help create personalized experiences and pitches. And you still need integrations that boost productivity by automating processes around the consistent flow of insightful data for CRM and CSM.

Many organizations employ third-party integration with their CIAM solution primarily as a way to use consumer data to enhance their marketing strategies. But every industry is different, and every business demands a different kind of **data sync**.

First, you have the choice of *two-way sync,* which pulls data from the third-party applications into consumer profiles in the CIAM system and sends profile data back to the application, or *one-way sync,* which pushes data from the source (CIAM) to the destination (third-party application). Then, you also have *real-time data sync,* which assures that new and altered data is automatically disseminated—instantly and consistently—to every third-party application integrated with your CIAM platform. Finally, there is what's called *historical data sync,* where historical consumer data is fed to third-party applications (marketers) to help them understand the consumer journey so they can build better sales pitches and marketing strategies.

Clearly, data syncing is more important than ever, with cloud-based data now so much more accessible—especially to mobile devices, which leverage it for basic operations. In this context, flawless syncing is crucial to keep sensitive information securely managed, stored, and transferred.

The good news: Proper implementation of this kind of data sync between a CIAM and third-party application can be a game changer for you and your business, impacting everything from marketing team productivity to order management to timely transportation to inventory management to cost efficiency.

In fact, the benefits from integrating third-party applications with your CIAM solution involve everything from smart data analytics (using data collected by your CIAM for insights into business processes) to data accessibility and error resolution (simplifying data accessibility and improving error handling, especially when a consumer onboards) to creating familiar and user-friendly environments (through seamless integrations with the applications consumers are already using in their day-to-day lives).

OMNICHANNEL

When we talk about an omnichannel consumer experience, we mean the consumer can be anywhere—on your websites on their desktop, on your mobile apps on their mobile phone, in a brick-and-mortar store—and still enjoy a coordinated, consistent experience throughout the journey.

Key capabilities of omnichannel support include:

- **Data management.** By breaking down silos and making data accessible across all service distribution channels, omnichannel support provides a helpful overview of consumers' whole data landscape.
- **A single admin panel.** This overall data landscape is conveyed with a single dashboard view for consumers' data, uniting all channels into one seamless admin panel.
- **A 360-degree view.** With this unified view of consumers' data, businesses can now manage everything—transactions, privacy settings, permissions, preferences, and consent—all at once.

> An omnichannel consumer experience is a multifold approach to marketing, selling, and supporting consumers across multiple physical and digital touchpoints.

USER MANAGEMENT

Finally, one of CIAM's essential components, of course, involves businesses' ability to manage and control consumers' access to various systems, devices, applications, and other resources.

Any solution designed to serve multiple consumers must have the following features:

- **Provisioning:** the ability to create new accounts
- **Authorization:** the ability to validate the access rights of consumers
- **Password management:** the ability to manage password resets for consumer accounts
- **Account management:** the ability to disable, grant, or restrict access for consumers
- **Deprovisioning:** the ability to block or delete consumer accounts
- **Data filtration:** the ability to search consumers based on different parameters like name, email, Universal ID (UID), ID, and phone ID
- **Data migration:** the ability to migrate existing consumer data from multiple sources
- **Real-time data feeds:** the ability to provide consumer data in real time using webhooks and APIs

WHAT COMES NEXT

In this chapter, we looked at all the key capabilities of CIAM that can help bring consumers closer to your business.

Now that you have a clear picture of CIAM—as not just a technology platform (like IAM) but a *complete solution*—it's time to dial in on your own CIAM selection and design framework so that you can figure out what option works best for your business.

CHAPTER FOURTEEN

CIAM SELECTION AND DESIGN FRAMEWORK

We touched on this briefly in Chapter Nine, but now that we have come to the point of having to make some important decisions—about how to best design your own CIAM system—we must take a closer look at the question of **on-premises vs. cloud-based** deployment.

If your business involves serving your customers online, these are your two choices to manage their digital identities: Either you can download the software for your CIAM solution and install it yourself, running it on your own server/hardware, or you can go for a cloud-based CIAM.

Ultimately, the ball is in your court. You need to decide, first, what is most important to your business and then, conversely, what you can afford to sacrifice. We will explain all this further in the following pages.

> What is your primary driver? Is it cost or performance?

Take the time to learn about all the options, define the distinct requirements of your organization, and then choose the solution that best fits your needs.

What are the pros and cons of each? Let's start by exploring the on-premises solution (or "on-prem," as it's called in the industry).

ON-PREM CIAM DEPLOYMENT

This is just what it sounds like. It means you host your CIAM platform on your company's own premises. Doing so gives you full control over all the platforms, applications, systems, and data related to your consumer identity management.

You own and operate the entire infrastructure, from physical computing and storage resources to server models and network switches.

On-prem deployment is commonly used in environments where the data is deemed too sensitive to be transmitted through public networks or where the transfer of such data outside of a private network is prohibited by local regulations.

Clearly, there are a lot of advantages to on-prem. You retain complete control of your data and can customize every part of the identity management process. It's also very secure: Because the entire infrastructure is on your own premises, there's little chance of third-party interference.

But there are also real drawbacks to consider. If you host your CIAM solution on premises, naturally that means it's also your organization's responsibility to *maintain* it. Do your people have the IT skills to not just set up your identity management system but to keep it going in the long run? Can they ensure that it will work as planned and integrate with your other systems?

Our purpose here isn't to scare you but to *tell it like it is*, and the truth is that the process with on-premises deployment is inherently complicated. **To pull it off, your company has to have the right personnel who possess the right expertise**—not just the skills to configure the setup but a depth of knowledge and experience in identity management and security work.

If you go the on-prem route, you should expect to add long-term expenses to your IT budget.

When it comes to the costs of an on-prem solution, you'll need to factor in the ongoing improvement and maintenance. Just be aware that having to consistently add new features and integrations (or keep existing ones updated) can be a real challenge for a lot of companies.

If you lack the technical expertise or resources to implement new or updated features, this will have a profoundly detrimental effect, not just on your ability to collect meaningful data but on the whole consumer experience.

So, if you are considering building your own on-prem CIAM solution but are feeling unsure whether it's right for you, ask yourself the following questions.

QUESTIONS	RESPONSE
What size of team do we need?	
How long will it take us to implement a robust solution?	
Can we keep up with technical and compliance changes as part of our ongoing operation?	
Do we have expertise available immediately in case something goes wrong?	
Can we afford all the implementation, testing, and support costs?	
Can we afford to divert resources aware of our core competencies?	
Can we produce an interoperable system that is faster, better, or cheaper than a bought solution?	
Do we have the resources to follow changes in the legal landscape around personal data management?	
Do we have the resources to follow and react to security developments in the various related protocols?	

How did you score? Before you make any decisions, read on—as we now turn our attention to the pros and cons of cloud-based solutions.

CLOUD-BASED CIAM DEPLOYMENT

How exactly does this differ from on-prem deployment? In a cloud environment, of course, a third-party provider hosts everything for you. A cloud-based server uses virtual technology to host your applications offsite.

The beauty is that you pay for this part on an as-needed basis; you can effectively scale up or down at your own pace, based on factors like overall usage, user requirements, and company growth.

Furthermore, because it is already configured, a cloud-based environment offers almost immediate upgrading. When a new product is introduced, it becomes available right away.

With a cloud-based deployment, you can of course also *back up* your data on a regular schedule. Moreover, it enables you to communicate with clients, partners, and other companies with little effort.

Still not sure if this solution makes sense for you? Keep in mind that **the cloud has much greater potential for organizations pursuing ambitious growth on a global scale.**

With a cloud-based CIAM solution, there are no capital expenses, and you only pay for what you use.

If you decide to go this route, you also need to make a choice about whether to use a single-tenant or multi-tenant cloud architecture. What's the difference?

Single-tenant cloud runs on a dedicated infrastructure. That means that the hardware, storage, and network are dedicated to a single client; you don't have to share hosted resources with any neighbors.

Multi-tenant, on the other hand, refers to a single cloud architecture that is built to serve multiple businesses. In other words, the system may cover a lot of different servers and data centers, but resources are shared among clients.

Let's look a little closer at how each works and what the pros and cons are:

SINGLE-TENANT CLOUD

First, it is important to understand that with a single-tenant cloud, the infrastructure may reside either in a dedicated offsite data center or with a managed private cloud provider. But no matter what, you get your own cloud environment, and your data remains separate from other tenants.

Single-tenant architecture is also built in such a way that only one software instance per software-as-a-service (SaaS) server is allowed. When you become a new tenant, a new piece of software is purpose-built for you. You can even configure your user interface (UI) after the installation is complete.

Here's how it works: **After your single-tenant environment is set up, you configure it to better fit your specific CIAM needs.** You can also choose when to install any available upgrades; you don't have to wait for the service provider.

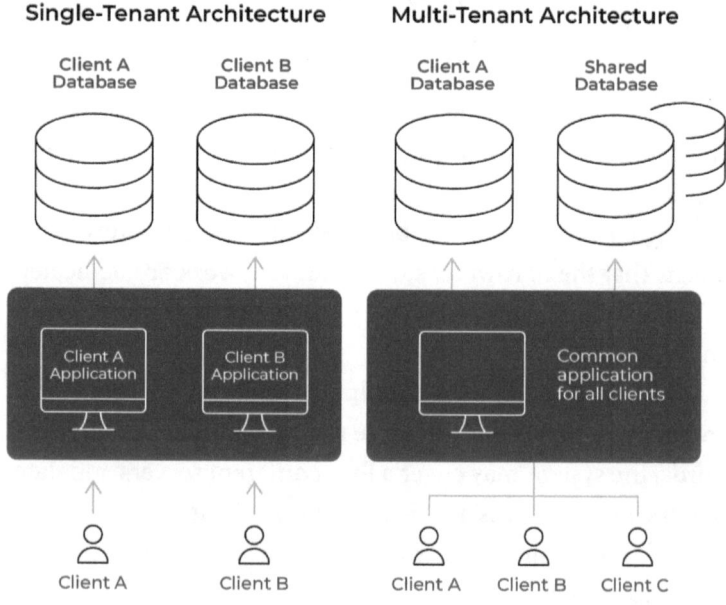

Image source: netsolutions.com

The advantages of a single-tenant cloud solution are largely self-evident. There is the enhanced *security* that comes with true data isolation. You don't have the same risk of data leakage between tenants that can happen (either unintentionally or by sabotage) in a multi-tenant environment. For this reason, single-tenant design is a common option for large corporations looking for optimal protection.

As we've just learned, single tenancy also gives companies the ability to *customize* their configuration because the software is unique to them and can be modified. This also applies to network and storage infrastructure: Single tenancy carries the ability to architect one's environment as needed, with control over variables like the amount of memory required, the type of network switching (to serve traffic), or the local and external storage solutions for best meeting capacity and performance needs.

Similarly, single tenancy offers much more flexibility when it comes to *upgrades*. Again, rather than having to wait for the software provider to launch a universal update, you can upgrade your services individually. Accounts can be updated as soon as the download is available, at your individual convenience.

A single-tenant cloud solution is also very *reliable*. Because you're using an application that isn't affected by other tenants, you have a very high and very consistent level of performance. As the only user, all resources in the environment belong to you, which means that intensive applications (demanding consistently high performance) have a higher chance of being met.

Having a dedicated infrastructure—that doesn't divide resources like with a multi-tenant approach—also allows for *easy restoration and backup*. With an isolated backup of your database, it's much easier for you and your team to access historical information and restore previous settings.

Finally, a single-tenant infrastructure makes *migration* very smooth and easy. If or when you want to migrate into a self-hosted or local environment, you can quickly move an application to your own managed servers.

So, given all those benefits, why would you possibly decide against a single-tenant SaaS cloud architecture?

Like with anything, there are also drawbacks, and one of the main downsides of this approach is *cost*. **Single-tenant doesn't allow for any cost-sharing with deployment and monitoring.** You pay more than you would if costs were shared among multiple tenants.

> Single-tenant cloud architecture is usually more expensive because it requires more maintenance and is more challenging to set up.

So, how does a multi-tenant cloud solution fare when it comes to these factors?

MULTI-TENANT CLOUD

Think of multi-tenant like an apartment building. Each resident is allowed access to their own unit, but they share utilities like electricity and water, as well as common areas like the rooftop. Similarly, cloud providers that offer multi-tenancy set the overall rules and performance standards for the different businesses but give you private access to your individual information.

With multi-tenancy, cloud providers share the same application with multiple businesses on the same hardware, in the same operational environment, and with the same storage mechanism.

Again, the main advantage of multi-tenant architecture has to do with cost. Simply put, it *saves money* because computing is cheaper at scale. Multi-tenancy allows resources to be consolidated and allocated efficiently, which cuts down the operational expenditures. And for that reason, paying for access to a cloud service or SaaS application is often more cost-effective than running single-tenant hardware and software.

Moreover, if you're invested in your own hardware and software, you run the risk of reaching capacity during times of high demand and, conversely, sitting idle during low-demand periods. But with multi-tenant cloud, there is much more *flexibility*: You can access extra capacity when you need it and not pay for it when you don't. The cloud provider allocates a pool of resources as the needs of their different tenants scale up and down.

Multi-tenancy is also *efficient*: It reduces the need for you to manage infrastructure and handle updates and maintenance. You don't have to rely on your own teams to handle those routine chores. The central cloud provider does it all.

Finally, multi-tenant architecture is great for *scalability*. Onboarding users with these platforms is a cinch. It is easy to manage any demand, and the system is not vulnerable to overloads like with single-tenancy.

A cloud multi-tenant architecture may have a significant impact on the deployment of software and services. It gives organizations unparalleled reliability, accessibility, and scalability—while facilitating cost savings.

That said, multi-tenant platforms are actually more vulnerable, not less, from a *security* standpoint. Cybercriminals can take advantage of multiple access points to exploit the systems' vulnerabilities.

Another drawback of multi-tenant cloud architecture is its inferior *backup and restoration* capacities. Most multi-tenant platforms don't offer robust restoration options, and it is easy to fall behind with the latest system backup advances.

Multi-tenant also doesn't provide a lot of *customization* options like single-tenant does. This limits how much control you have over the quality of the environment and ability to interact with the system.

Last, there is the problem of *concurrent issues*, meaning that when a multi-tenant cloud provider makes a change to the core software, all tenants are affected. This can hinder uptime, system upgrades, and more.

CHAPTER FIFTEEN

CIAM BEST PRACTICES

CIAM helps organizations to both provide great consumer experiences *and* be protected against fraud, breaches, and privacy violations.

As for the first part of that formulation, we have seen how CIAM helps brands connect the dots from various consumer touchpoints to create a cohesive experience and a seamless journey for omnichannel shoppers.

By allowing for a single unified view of consumer profiles, CIAM helps build the foundation for multi-channel experiences and customized interactions. A comprehensive CIAM platform brings together all data—including the identity information, purchasing histories, and use and buying patterns in each consumer profile—and uses it for boosting revenue, personalized marketing, and new product development.

As we've learned, APIs are also used extensively in CIAM to incorporate identity data and analytics into complementary frameworks (such as content management, ERP, and consumer experience management).

Finally, CIAM creates a great consumer experience by providing users with a seamless registration process—which they can complete on multiple devices and across multiple channels—including social login (such as via Google or Facebook). If further authentication is required, CIAM provides low-friction methods (such as passwordless authentication that is either email-based, SMS-based, or biometric).

> Let your CIAM solution unlock the door to boosting revenue, personalized marketing, and new product development.

With CIAM, gone are the days of consumer dissatisfaction (and potentially lost sales) from registration fatigue and frustrating digital experiences. **Companies that know how to leverage the power of CIAM will win the next wave of consumer delight.**

But equally important is how CIAM helps organizations ensure compliance with local and global regulations, which in turn creates trust and transparency with consumers.

Virtually all companies these days are responsible for securely collecting, managing, analyzing, and protecting consumer data. But it can be difficult to capture and safely store this data. CIAM addresses this problem by creating unified profiles. It also helps to give the modern consumer what they want and expect, namely more control over their own personal data and how it is being used.

With CIAM, companies have the peace of mind that they are doing right with *everyone*: not just their customers and not just the government regulators to whom compliance is now ensured, but also the stakeholders in their own business. That's because their business assets are now better protected.

According to EMA research, 60 percent of all businesses experience security breaches each year, and 90 percent of those affected report severe consequences, including loss of revenue, loss of consumer trust, fines, and remediation costs.[25]

Your CIAM solution brings with it—by virtue of its adherence to all the major security assurance programs—the confidence of knowing that consumer accounts aren't being used to conduct criminal activities like fraud and identity theft.

If you are a business that offers paid services, your identity solution helps ensure that no one is bypassing security to use those services for free.

Even with all these assurances, however, it's worth remembering that there will *always* be a balance you have to navigate between security and consumer experience—and in the following pages we'll explore the various practices and common trade-offs that will help you best find that sweet spot.

BUILDING THE RIGHT BALANCE BETWEEN SECURITY AND CONSUMER EXPERIENCE

How can your organization capture the healthy middle ground between security and experience—keeping your consumers' data safe while still providing them with the most seamless journey?

---

25 "Advancing Identity and Access Management to the Next Level with Contextual Awareness," Enterprise Management Associates, accessed June 25, 2024, https://info.enterprisemanagement.com/identity-and-access-management-2020-webinar-pr.

Where you land on this question can make a huge difference to your bottom line and in some cases your very survival. **Achieving the right balance means generating greater business opportunities and dramatically reducing the potential of being hacked.**

McKinsey & Company lay out a number of important considerations when it comes to negotiating these delicate trade-offs between experience and security. First, when it comes to the control area of having a single identifier for each customer, you must identify the most important use cases—and from there determine whether to take a more experience-driven approach and focus on improving business analytics or a more security-forward approach that prioritizes stronger account monitoring. The same careful balance is required with other control areas, like multifactor authentication, where you should certainly offer a mix of MFA options but only in combination with other more secure identity-proofing techniques.[26]

---

[26] Tucker Bailey et al., "Building Security into the Customer Experience," McKinsey & Company, June 29, 2020, https://www.mckinsey.com/capabilities/risk-and-resilience/our-insights/building-security-into-the-customer-experience.

Trade-offs should be considered carefully to preserve security while promoting a positive customer experience.

Sample trade-offs between customer experience and security by control area

Control	Experience-driven approach	Experience-driven approach	Experience-driven approach
Single identifier for each customer	Emphasize customization, with customer service based on associated behavior pattern	Focus on user behavior analytics to refine account monitoring for abnormalities or fraud	Utilize a single identifier for each customer and identify priority use cases to determine whether to improve business analytics or build stronger account monitoring
Multifactor authentication (MFA)	Offer many options for MFA, including voice or text messages, email factors, biometrics, and pattern recognition	Enforce use of highly secure MFA methods, including tokens or device recognition and biometrics; combine with identity-proofing techniques	Offer a mix of MFA options in addition to identity-proofing techniques; if needed, suggest a more secure MFA to avoid reauthentication
Reauthentication	Limit need for reauthentication by only requiring MFA for specific transactions (e.g., updating billing payment) *Or*	Require reauthentication for each transaction to ensure the user's identity remains unchanged throughout the session	Use triggers for reauthentication when abnormal behavior is detected (such as many attempts to reset a password) and require reauthentication for highly sensitive transactions (e.g., resetting a billing method)
Look out policies	Allow users five or more attempts to provide credentials before account lock occurs requiring administrative support	Allow only one or two attempts to reduce risk of brute-force attacks despite need for administrative support	Allow three attempts and impose a "soft lock" (e.g., need identity-proofing) before requiring administrative support
Session policies	Enable longer session times to allow users to perform several transactions without timing out	Limit session time to a minimum, allowing users to refresh tokens if session extension is needed	Designate session times based on a user group's needs (e.g., in healthcare, doctors and administrators may need longer sessions than patients)

Source: McKinsey & Company

Putting forth the option of a more secure MFA means generally avoiding having to ask users to reauthenticate. But if reauthentication does become necessary, a good way to address these sometimes dueling imperatives of experience and security is to limit reauthentication to scenarios involving highly sensitive transactions (like resetting a building method) or abnormal user behavior (like multiple attempts to reset a password).

Traditionally, when users provide the wrong credentials

multiple times in a row, they are locked out of their account. But how many attempts should they get? An experience-driven approach gives them many chances (five or more), whereas a more security-forward approach reduces the risk of brute-force attacks by allowing only one or two. McKinsey recommends a happy medium of three attempts and then a "soft lock" that just requires identity-proofing rather than administrative support.

Finally, there are the questions of how long session times should last and how many transactions users should be allowed to perform before they time out. Again, there is a healthy middle ground here where organizations can designate session times based on the distinct needs of different user *groups*. For example, in the healthcare arena, doctors and administrators probably need longer sessions than patients.

The goal with all these control areas, of course, is to never have to sacrifice security for consumer experience, or vice versa—and CIAM is what makes it possible to have your proverbial cake and eat it too.

But that can only happen if you maintain best practices with your CIAM, not only for your consumers—who expect an easy and seamless interaction—but so that you can protect their identity while regulating access.

ADAPTING TO THE NEW CONSUMER EXPERIENCE REALITY

We've talked a lot here about trade-offs. But when all is said and done, the real beauty of a CIAM solution lies in its focus on enhancing the consumer experience without having to compromise security.

We know that 69 percent of today's consumers are concerned about their personal data and what happens to it.[27] They are looking for secure registration, but they are also looking for frictionless experiences, easy login, and seamless transactions.

According to KPMG's 3rd Global Customer Experience Excellence report, the strongest factor in driving consumer loyalty (in nineteen of the twenty-seven markets covered in the report) is *personalization*. In six of the markets, *integrity* was seen as the most important.

Integrity is also especially important when it comes to driving advocacy, which is measured by the Net Promoter Score (NPS).

In adapting to these new consumer priorities, organizations need to be constantly rethinking their business and operating models—**investing in new digital methods for communications and payments while always staying focused on digital security.**

The good news is that your CIAM solution lets you do just that, using detailed data about your consumer's ongoing interactions with your brand—everything they have done since the first time they visited your website or app—to monitor their journey across multiple applications and services, design new products or special offers, and facilitate other multi-channel personalization to drive revenue and loyalty.

CIAM gives you a practical path not only to this important *centralization* of consumer identity but to the challenge of staying ahead of cybersecurity and the ever-changing privacy laws.

---

27 "The Trust Opportunity: Exploring Consumer Attitudes to the Internet of Things," Internet Society, May 1, 2019, https://www.internetsociety.org/resources/doc/2019/trust-opportunity-exploring-consumer-attitudes-to-iot/.

ADAPTING TO THE NEW REALITY OF PRIVACY AND SECURITY

With new privacy laws being implemented worldwide, and more on the way, businesses *must, must, must* stay on top of these regulations. This is where CIAM comes in and helps by:

- Maintaining evidence of how, when, where, and why consumer data is obtained and processed;
- Providing transparency on how businesses gather and use consumers' personal data;
- Addressing all demands of data privacy regulations on your consumer-facing applications;
- Implementing a holistic approach to consumer profile management and consent;
- Ensuring effective regulation of consent and expectations by centralizing and streamlining data governance;
- Reducing costs and IT complexity through a single platform's control of digital identities, authentication, and authorization; and
- Protecting businesses from regulatory threats by safeguarding confidential data and intellectual property.

To be clear, it's not only the privacy regulations that are evolving at a manic rate. So is cybersecurity itself. With cybercriminals getting smarter and faster with every data breach, protecting consumer data has become more of a demanding challenge than ever before. *Keeping up* with cybersecurity is now an absolute necessity.

Thankfully, as we've learned, powerful CIAM solutions give us the tools—such as single sign-on, multifactor authentication, and adaptive authentication—to ensure our consumers can engage with us *securely* at any time and from any device.

> Cybersecurity technology has evolved exponentially. So have the devious methods of cybercriminals.

For example, companies pursuing a *zero trust model* (which we described back in Chapter Thirteen) must keep in mind capabilities like adaptive authentication and dark web monitoring.

We haven't talked much in this book about the dark web, but everyone knows that the anonymity of the dark web makes it a hotspot for illegal activities. It is almost impossible in this environment to identify criminal locations without access to closed sources, specialized knowledge, and technology that's capable of monitoring sources that misuse data.

Dark web monitoring is a great example of how cybersecurity has evolved and become incredibly sophisticated. It offers round-the-clock surveillance to detect compromised digital credentials.

With dark web monitoring, consumer data is also encrypted and routed through multiple servers around the world, making it extremely difficult for hackers to track.

WHAT COMES NEXT

Over the past few chapters, hopefully you've come to possess a clear picture of CIAM's key capacities, options for design, and best practices for experience and security. Now, it's time to start *preparing your case.* That means going back to the different teams and individuals you spoke to earlier—in Chapter Eight—when you were asking questions and gathering information.

But this time, the goal is to mobilize and onboard them in

preparation for implementation. **Each department will have a different role, and everyone will understand who is going to own what part of the implementation.**

You will also be mobilizing *resources.* Resource planning is a key element at this stage: What resources are going to be required to implement?

Ultimately, you'll emerge with a clear understanding of the interactions and roles of the different departments within your organization and who's going to do what. You'll have your strategy, your execution plan, and your technological case for the CIAM solution you advocate.

But what about the **business case**?

If you're going to be asking for, say, $2 million from the finance department, you'll need to have all your ducks in a row. This means researching vendors, studying all the benefits of your solution, and analyzing the ROI—which is what Part Four is all about.

PART FOUR

CIAM

A Growth Driver

CHAPTER SIXTEEN

SEEING THE BENEFITS

At this stage in your journey, not only do you finally understand the ins and outs of the digital identity challenges your company is facing, but you also have a firm grasp on how a CIAM solution can be used to solve it.

What now?

You'll need to have a strategy on how to pitch this all to management—and make a business case that, by putting such-and-such amount of money toward the solution, **you'll reap the benefits of engagement, conversion, cost-savings**, and more.

Before you go to your CEO or CFO with your use case, you'll also need to look at what *other* companies (and other industries) have done—and how they've benefited.

But first, in order to understand all the ways a brand can benefit, let's examine how exactly the end-users will be better served:

USER BENEFITS OF CIAM

As it relates to the user, the most important benefit is that you will now be able to deliver to them a truly **modern customer experience**. What does that mean exactly? Above all, the difference now is that it's a *unified* experience. This is because you've centralized all customer services, such as subscription, support, billing, booking, account updates, purchasing, and refunds.

Furthermore, the experience is *seamless*: Customers use a single identity and single profile at all touchpoints, with all digital properties and brands—which makes for what we could also describe as a *connected* experience, on mobile apps and IoT/smart devices such as TVs and gaming consoles.

Importantly, it's not just the general user experience that's been modernized but also the *onboarding* experience, through social login, passwordless login, and phone login. Customer profiles are automatically created using social login.

What about security? With your new CIAM solution, **your ability to protect users' accounts and data has, of course, greatly increased.** How so? First, as it relates to their accounts, due to the increased level of protection around digital assets such as apps and websites, the authentication process—to make sure users have the authority to access these digital properties—has been greatly strengthened.

You are now able to enforce stronger security through the most up-to-date, state-of-the-art industry encryption, password policies, and signature and IP-based controls.

Advanced security monitoring allows you to lock down accounts if there are aberrations and send user notifications or alerts regarding unusual activity.

In terms of securing user data, not only is your compliance with regional security regulations now guaranteed, but you are also protected from spam account creation during registration.

The *consistency* of user data is also now assured, so you won't see all the random information and garbage you used to. We call this "data sanity."

Finally, the protocols around security that developers use in their software and implementation have now automatically been brought in line with industry standards.

As for privacy, the **increased privacy compliance helps to not only reduce liability but also build customer trust.**

How exactly is privacy compliance strengthened? Your new solution manages user consent flawlessly, which ensures compliance with regional data privacy regulations. It also helps ensure compliance with storage regulation through global data centers.

COST BENEFITS TO YOUR ORGANIZATION

Part of your business case must, of course, also include a discussion of revenue growth and cost reduction.

First, there is no question whatsoever—and you can tell this to your revenue department—that the optimization of your marketing efforts will have the effect of increasing revenue. Here's how: By centralizing customer identity, gaining a new unified view of your user, and making data available to various systems through integrations, you'll now be able to upsell and cross-sell to them.

As we saw with the earlier example of *Vogue* and GQ—or for that matter, Google—upselling and cross-selling increases customer engagement, ultimately raising the average revenue per user.

> Unleash the power of customer data with integrations.

Not only will you now see higher engagement, satisfaction, and retention, but the simplified registration and new potential for progressive profiling will also increase user conversion.

Finally, **the simplified implementation created by your new CIAM solution will significantly reduce the costs associated with IT and engineering.**

Assuming you don't try to host your product on premises (it carries extensive challenges, as we saw in Chapter Fourteen, and is ill-advised for most readers), your solution won't require any development, just configuration. This allows you to implement and go to market that much quicker.

Furthermore, if you go with a cloud solution, which (again) is what we recommend in the vast majority of cases, everything will be fully managed. This includes auto-scaling—which, as you grow, will allow you to handle millions of users and backups and avoid the headaches that come with administration, uptime, and latency.

All in all, the total cost of ownership (TCO) for you when it comes to identity management will be vastly reduced.

You'll have lower costs for your IT infrastructure. Because your CIAM solution already factors in everything related to infrastructure cost and maintenance, you won't have to host or manage application servers and IT components anymore.

Moreover, your **new maintenance-free solution will save you money on security and upgrades.**

Finally, because you're not trying to implement customer identity on premises—which would require at least four or five engineers and probably many more—you will now save money by cutting your engineering resources, as we'll see in the following section.

> CIAM will reduce your total cost of ownership (TCO) around identity management.

DEPARTMENTAL BENEFITS

In addition to eliminating research and development (R & D) costs with an out-of-the-box CIAM solution, and not having to manage the cloud infrastructure to run the software, there is also the benefit to your engineering department of not having to *maintain the software* either. If a bug is detected or an enhancement is needed or a security breach occurs (or really, any such issue), the engineering team doesn't need to do anything because the cloud CIAM vendor handles it.

Moreover, because there is always so much evolution and innovation happening in the identity space, the engineering team can leave *all of that* to the CIAM vendor and instead focus on their bread and butter: enhancing their own product features to stay ahead of the curve in the ever-expanding competitive digital landscape.

But it's not just the engineering department that benefits from an out-of-the-box CIAM solution. When it comes to your *security* team, having a modern cloud solution in place can be a game changer for a department exhausted by the enormous challenge of having to secure heaps of sensitive and confidential information about their business and consumers. Your CIAM vendor will handle staying up to date with all specific industry standards, leaving you (and your personnel tasked with managing security/risk) much less prone to breaches and data leaks.

As for your privacy/legal department, they too benefit from your cloud-based CIAM solution: Now they can sleep well at night knowing they are staying compliant with ever-changing data privacy laws and regulations around the world. This is no small thing, considering the legal consequences (and potential for further investigations and fines) of not paying adequate attention to such matters.

Not only does an out-of-the-box CIAM solution simplify data privacy compliance by bringing all consumer data under one roof, so to speak, but it satisfies byzantine regional laws by ensuring the data is stored locally in different cloud servers within the physical boundaries of each state or country. It also fulfills the essential requirements of data privacy laws around centralized user management and MFA, as well as data encryption, data access control, and consent management.

Finally, your cloud-based CIAM solution will of course, as we've already seen, benefit your marketing/revenue department by leveraging personalization to enhance the user experience—and ultimately foster greater trust among your end users. Trust, in turn, is the gateway to more sales, more effective marketing, and overall revenue growth. We've seen time and again how CIAM, implemented strategically within any business model, eventually maximizes conversion rates, turning leads into customers, and reduces consumer abandonment. Finally, specific CIAM features like progressive profiling can help businesses capture user information gradually, in steps, which is incredibly useful for marketing, as it can be used in real time to derive leads through personalized experiences and produce recommendations.

GETTING BUY-IN FROM ALL QUARTERS

Clearly, your CIAM solution is going to help *everyone*: not just your external users, but also your internal teams, from engineering to security to legal to marketing. **The benefits are different depending on who's looking at this new reality, and from what angle.** But once you and your people see what it will do across the board for each and every department, you'll realize that the impact—in every corner of your org chart—is a positive one.

Still, you'll need to be educated and prepared to answer questions, not just from your CFO but anyone from any area of your business. Maybe your security officer has concerns, or your customer service team.

Be ready to defend your business case with itemized forecasts.

Obviously, nobody can read the future. But what you *can* do is make logical projections around benefits based on what other companies have seen. Do your research about competitors in the same space who have adopted these solutions. Also look outside your industry for parallels that can provide insights.

The more specific you can be, the better. Ultimately, you're going to want to have done the math and be able to make the case that what you are proposing will save your company millions of dollars a year.

The good news is that there has been a sea change in the way cyber risks are viewed within organizations: Finally, executives and board directors are seeing cybersecurity as a critical component of their business strategy.

Seem obvious: After all, when a cybercriminal strikes, that person takes away much more than consumer data. It can be a huge blow to a company's bottom line and brand reputation.

But until recently, cyber risks were viewed as highly *technical* threats, which made it hard to get buy-in from all the important organizational stakeholders. Nowadays, thankfully, companies realize it takes equal effort from all parties.

In particular, CIOs (chief information officers), CMOs (chief marketing officers), and DPOs (data protection officers) need to work together, leveraging their roles to better understand, align with, and protect their consumers.

Let's look a little closer at how these different individuals must each play a part:

CIOs are obliged to turn new technologies into revenue. CMOs are on the front line of dealing with brand value and consumer data. And DPOs look to find security and privacy loopholes within an enterprise.

In particular, collaboration between the marketing and engineering departments is key to boosting productivity, driving digital transformation across the enterprise, mapping and aligning business needs with stakeholder demands, and planning and modeling the future.

As for DPOs, they are expected to:

- Keep the organization and its employees current about the newly evolved data protection laws.
- Monitor the organization's compliance obligations and adhere to global data protection regulation.
- Function as the point of contact for other organizational stakeholders like the CMO and CIO.

No wonder DPOs, CIOs, and CMOs are finally seeing themselves as the natural partners that they are.

Even with this positive trend, however, you are still going to have to draw on your research and experience to build a convincing proposal for all the decision makers—one that you'll also be able to use to answer individual questions across the company.

So far, so good.

But how, ultimately, will you measure your ongoing success against your current forecasts? How will you know if your solution is having the success you predicted?

You have to define your own ROI.

CHAPTER SEVENTEEN

DEFINING YOUR OWN ROI

Why is ROI so important?

If you made a business case for CIAM without defining your own success metrics, then you're not going to be able to measure how well it's working. How will you know where to look for growth?

Take, for example, user experience. According to the Big Four accounting group KPMG, "Even when organizations develop business cases for customer experience, many fail to ground their investment plans on financial/customer measures with a clear linkage to value generation."[28]

Moreover, if you haven't explicitly articulated your ROI, or don't have a system in place for tracking the progress, how will you know if something needs to change or be tweaked?

As we'll see in this chapter, user experience metrics can

---

28 Julio Hernandez, *How Much Is Customer Experience Worth?* (KPMG, September 2016), https://assets.kpmg.com/content/dam/kpmg/xx/pdf/2016/11/How-much-is-custerom-experience-worth.pdf.

vary by business. There are **some metrics like this that are industry-specific, but others are more general.** Revenue, privacy, security, and engineering metrics, for example, are the same for everyone.

To understand what we mean by industry-specific metrics, think about an e-commerce business versus a media company. The two would likely use very different metrics.

For the e-commerce outfit, it's all about *sales*: How many users are buying from their website, how many items have they sold, and how much revenue has it all generated?

For the media company, it's a different story: Because they're not being paid directly by their users—consumers aren't actually buying anything from them—the metrics that matter are *ads*, how many people clicked on the ads and how much revenue was generated.

Of course, the media company may have a subscription model, like a magazine. In that case, the important metrics are how many new subscribers they get and how many page views they get from free users. They may also care about **monetizing the data gathered from their subscribers**—and to do that, they need to stay on top of their metrics.

It goes to show that metrics aren't just about the degree to which your ROI has been achieved or surpassed—it's about applying that knowledge toward your bottom line.

As KPMG puts it: "We recommend linking investments designed to repair experience shortfalls to specific customer activity measures such as attrition, repurchase rates, and/or customer lifetime value.

"*Such measures can then be translated into a financial impact.*"[29]

---

29 Hernandez, *How Much Is Customer Experience Worth?*

> What are the most important metrics for *your* business?

KEY METRICS

Once you deploy your CIAM solution, here are some of the metrics you'll need to track:

- Conversion: Sign-up rate, Revisit
- User satisfaction rate
- Increased revenue
- User engagement metrics such as page view or time spent
- Reduction in engineering and security spend

It's also important to be aware of certain metrics in your company that *won't* be affected by CIAM—which is to be expected and not a bad thing—so you don't mistake this data for failure.

YOUR HAPPINESS METRICS

One of the key tasks in this stage of defining your ROI is to identify those **metrics that you see as defining your way of life going forward as a business.**

What is your *happiness metric*? In other words, what does success look like for your company?

There are also happiness/success benefits on the external (user) side, but what we're talking about here has to do with the internal (employee) side: What is the desired ROI from the security team, for example? What will they feel—what will their new lives and roles in the company look like—in this new reality where they don't have to worry about managing the security of users' accounts and data themselves, or about staying on top of regional security regulations?

If you are a larger company, you've probably already gone through this project of defining your happiness/success ROIs, in addition to other metrics we've been discussing here. After all, if you hadn't already done so, you wouldn't have approved the CIAM initiative.

But if you are still building your case, be aware that when you are asking your company to put up two million dollars (or whatever the amount may be) toward this new strategy, **you will need to show them how, once invested and implemented, you plan to measure the impact and return.**

THE CADENCE OF METRIC ANALYSIS

You should also understand that when it comes to tracking the happiness and success of the different departments—and this is true of *all* the metrics discussed in this chapter—it's not as if you just determine your ROI has been achieved, and then that's that. It's not a one-and-done thing. **Analysis of metrics must happen on a regular monthly schedule**, and in a structured, combined way, so that your company can look at the success of its efforts from every angle.

Having internal discussions and interviews, on an ongoing basis, with key personnel from different departments—to see where they stand, vis-à-vis those happiness and other metrics that they originally established—goes a long way to creating a strong path for continuous growth and improvement.

If, however, you chose to build your own digital identity solution, that path can get quite complicated, as we'll see in the following chapter.

CHAPTER EIGHTEEN

BUILDING VS. BUYING

When it comes down to it, there are two or three different types of companies. First, you have the ones who *outsource everything*. They do that because they don't have a strong tech or engineering team; it's not their core business. So, whether they're buying new software or delegating their technical work to a third party, the name of the game with these kinds of organizations is **buying**.

Then, on the other side of the spectrum, you have the hardcore tech companies who bring a huge amount of talent and expertise to the engineering side.

But then there are those in the middle, who try to do some things in-house but don't completely discard outsourcing. That is mainly because they recognize their own limits. But they also still love developing new things and are always excited about opportunities to work on new projects.

So, when the question of building versus buying a CIAM solution comes to the forefront, often there's more going on behind the scenes than just an objective assessment of pros and cons. There's an emotional component.

Often, the engineering group pushes to build it themselves. Even though **studies show that this will cost the company more money, not less, in the long run**, there is an emotional attachment to doing things in-house that blurs the issue.

If your company is like the ones we've seen all too often, you're going to find that your engineers believe—or at least this is what they will argue—it will be easier, faster, and cheaper for *them* to build the CIAM.

But they're not the ones who will make the ultimate business decision. That responsibility lies with the C-suite folks and the CIO in particular. The finance department is also involved, of course. They look at the numbers and analyze risks and benefits.

Where do *you* fit into all of this?

There is a *process* that we encourage companies to use in assessing whether to build or buy.

By spearheading and championing this process, you can help ensure your company makes the right decision.

A PROCESS FOR ASSESSING BUILD-OR-BUY

For the purpose of this exercise, let's say you already know a few things about what you are looking for while deciding between build vs. buy.

You know you need *these* types of features, you know your website has *this* many million users, and so on. By using our assessment tool (in the link below[30]), all you have to do is plug in your inputs—it will then tell you how much building the

---

[30] "CIAM Build vs Buy," LoginRadius, accessed May 10, 2023, https://www.loginradius.com/resource/ciam-build-vs-buy/.

solution yourself is going to cost you and how much time it will take.

What we've seen, over and over, with companies who go through this process is that they come to **realize their in-house customer identity solution is either too expensive to maintain or no longer meets their needs (or both).**

Unfortunately, most companies *don't* do this kind of assessment before making a decision, and so they continue to pour resources into maintaining their in-house solution.

They're simply not aware of the shortcomings associated with this path. They don't know all that's going to be demanded of them. It's a lot: Obviously they'll need a development team. But not just that, the team will also constantly have to be chasing (or more likely playing catch-up) to stay up to date with the improvements and innovations that a good CIAM solution requires.

Now, contrast that with all the benefits that a modern CIAM platform would provide them, **all the value improvements, the quicker implementation time, and not to mention a significantly lower TCO.**

They wouldn't have to manage and maintain their customer identity solution and wouldn't have to hire new talent.

Yes, they might have to pay more up front, and certainly we encourage people to do their due diligence when it comes to cost.

But maybe instead of thinking about your purchased CIAM solution in terms of cost, you should be thinking in terms of *investment*. As you've seen throughout this book, consumer choice is higher than ever—and companies who provide a modern user experience while also protecting user data have a huge advantage over their competition.

When you start to look at it this way, you realize **the true**

investment value in *buying* (rather than building) lies in the improvements made to the overall functionality and security of your identity management.

To be clear, we're not saying it's *never* going to work to build a customer identity solution yourself. As explained at the beginning of the chapter, there are companies where this kind of work is their bread and butter. It's the right choice maybe 10 percent of the time—at most.

But even those kinds of organizations (the ones where it makes sense to build the solution themselves) must stay clear-eyed about everything that they're going to need to add on later.

No one is building identity from the ground up.

Your tech company has likely already sunk a lot of costs into your customer identity solution. It has already built what it built based on your business's specific requirements—and these initial requirements likely focused on key aspects linking authentication and registration.

Now, what happens when things change? When the company wants to add more applications? Or expand to other countries?

Unfortunately, what we tend to see is that **the resources the company already put into the initial cost of building the solution cannibalized its budget for maintenance and improvement.** What's worse, if it didn't define its ROI properly and hasn't been good about tracking its metrics, it probably doesn't even know how much its in-house solution has cost and is costing.

Not to beat a dead horse, but with an out-of-the-box solution, you don't have to worry about *any* of that.

It's all covered: maintenance costs, managed infrastructure, best practices, managed securities, and private compliances. Your purchased CIAM platform makes your life easier in almost every way. It's super easy now for you to sift through and segment your data, link to other applications, connect to your larger ecosystem—and in general grow, change, and adapt with your users.

It's an all-around better solution, and better *quality*, because you're hiring identity specialists. This isn't a knock on your engineers. They're great at what they're great at. In fact, why not free them up and let them work in their core competencies? Think of all the resources that could be redirected in new, strategic initiatives?

In summary, **buying is far cheaper, easier, and more secure than building CIAM in-house.**

Because your third-party, out-the-box CIAM solution is constantly being improved, it is inherently *future proof*!

Even though—hopefully by now—you've been persuaded by the wisdom of *buying*, our experience tells us you might still be feeling a kind of lingering, last-minute hesitation about it all.

Is that right?

Maybe you're thinking to yourself, *yeah, it makes sense, but I don't really want to be the* first *one out there doing it*. Maybe you're considering putting it off. *After all, why do I need to adopt the newest technology right away?*

As you'll see in the following chapter, you're *far* from the first or only one doing this. In fact, before long you'll probably be thinking, *Why didn't I do this sooner?*

CHAPTER NINETEEN

LEARNING FROM OTHERS

The majority of companies—including very large, very successful brands—have adopted and embraced the kind of CIAM solutions discussed in this book and are already experiencing the incredible benefits.

If you think you're going to be out there alone, in untested waters, think again.

Take, for example, one of our Fortune 500 clients. They are a Fortune 500 company but can better be described as a *group* of companies, serving consumers in places like Hong Kong, the Philippines, Macao, and China—all over the APAC region (Asia-Pacific)—where they own thirty-four brands, including retail, clothing, supermarkets, restaurants, and food chains.

The client had been operating all these brands separately, and it was creating a problem of identity silos and data silos. They wanted to make a change. We worked with their team and deployed a CIAM solution that created a single login, single identity, and single experience across all their brands.

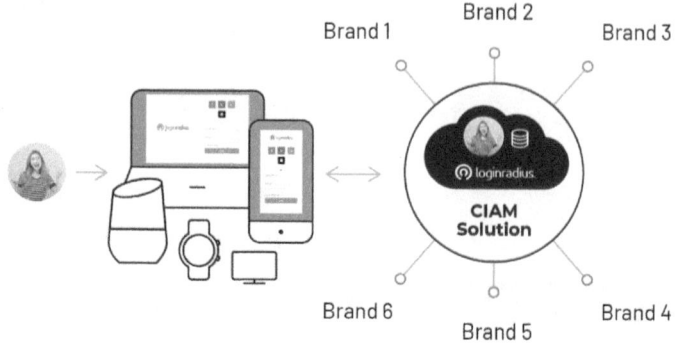

We took what was a broken experience and transformed it into a unified one. Not only was their data now centralized, enabling them to make better decisions, but this also opened up new doors for digital revenue.

A better user experience = more revenue.

The methodology we used with Jardine is pretty much exactly the same as what we have outlined for you in the previous chapters. We looked at how its different brands could be grouped together, identified common users, and analyzed its privacy needs in, say, China versus the Philippines.

Ultimately, because we helped Jardine deploy a modern, unified experience, it was able to retain users, reduce churn, and raise its signup rate. Moreover, because of the better, more inviting experience, users became increasingly digitally engaged.

Now, the company is also able to use the tools of cross-selling and upselling to take users who engage with one of its brands and try to extend that engagement to other Dairy Farm brands.

All in all, we love this example because it shows the direct impact that user experience can have on a company's revenue metrics.

But there are other equally impressive stories that highlight other metrics, such as scalability.

SCALING WITH CIAM

ITV is the second largest media house in the UK with $5 billion in annual revenue. They are made up of six different brands, and they came to us to help them create a centralized, personalized experience for their users. Their programming includes reality shows, and they have one show where they ask viewers to log in and vote for their favorite contestant. But within this short voting period—only two or three minutes—you have millions of people trying to log in, something like 10,000 logins per second.

Clearly, in delivering a CIAM solution to ITV, scalability was a very important factor. If the system broke during one of these peak-load events, it would be a disaster. How do you serve all those people in a span of just a few minutes? An internal system can't just auto-scale to a ten-times bigger server, or to ten more servers.

Scalability is one of many challenges that CIAM can solve.

For ITV, the most important metrics had to do with scaling and all the different aspects of scaling: numbers of users, number of data centers, number of applications, global coverage, and ability to handle peak loads.

In retrospect, the company is a model specimen for how CIAM enables scalability and is able to manage massively scalable systems.

But in this and other examples, we see too how CIAM's benefits are myriad. Scalability was key with ITV, but user experience has definitely contributed to their enduring success too.

As for security and privacy, those will always be strengthened by CIAM. In every scenario, this solution will allow you to better keep pace with the industry and its security and privacy protocols.

What are you waiting for?

Clearly, many other major companies have realized the power of CIAM.

This is not just a fleeting trend; it's already well underway.

Don't be the company that misses out. Be the company that's ahead of the curve—and you will rocket past your competition.

PART FIVE

THE FUTURE

CHAPTER TWENTY

BEING READY FOR THE FUTURE

If you're anything like us, there's a good chance you have an Amazon Alexa in your home. Smart speakers and other such technology—Google Home, etc.—have really taken off in recent years, as voice-activated experience has emerged as a consumer trend (as we saw in Chapter Four).

In fact, Amazon revealed that global purchases of Alexa-enabled devices surpassed 500 million in 2023.[31] But again, what's even more striking than the rate of adoption for these products is just how quickly we are seeing masses of consumers make the switch from keyboard search queries to using their voice.

---

31 Alexandra Garfinkle, "Amazon Has Sold More Than 500 Million Alexa-Enabled Devices, Drops 4 New Echo Products," Yahoo! Finance, May 17, 2023, https://finance.yahoo.com/news/amazon-has-sold-more-than-500-million-alexa-enabled-devices-drops-4-new-echo-products-140013808.html.

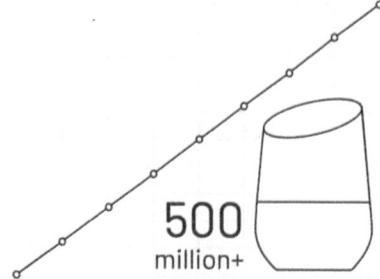

Amazon revealed that global purchases of Alexa-enabled devices surpassed 500 million in 2023

500 million+

Back in 2014, we wouldn't have known that something like an Alexa would have become so popular. In today's world, not only do these new technologies come at a rapid clip, but they also grow very fast. In contrast to medical science, for example, where something invented today might take twenty years to roll out, these innovations in voice recognition or facial recognition are being embraced by consumers very quickly and on a wide scale.

Clearly, this has big implications when it comes to identity. With CIAM, it's not about just inventing a new way of logging in or authenticating. It's also about consumer behavior: The new method needs to be adopted by the lion's share of users.

This means that you need to stay focused on not just the evolution of technology but also on how people are responding to and using these tools to interact with different interfaces. If you take your eye off the ball on the market side, you could fall behind and ultimately hurt your business.

Already, people are logging into their laptops, tablets, and mobile phones by just speaking, or with facial recognition. Three years from now, most of us are likely not going to be using passwords at all. At that point, authentication will involve a combination of voice ID, face ID, and biometrics (which we will discuss later in this chapter).

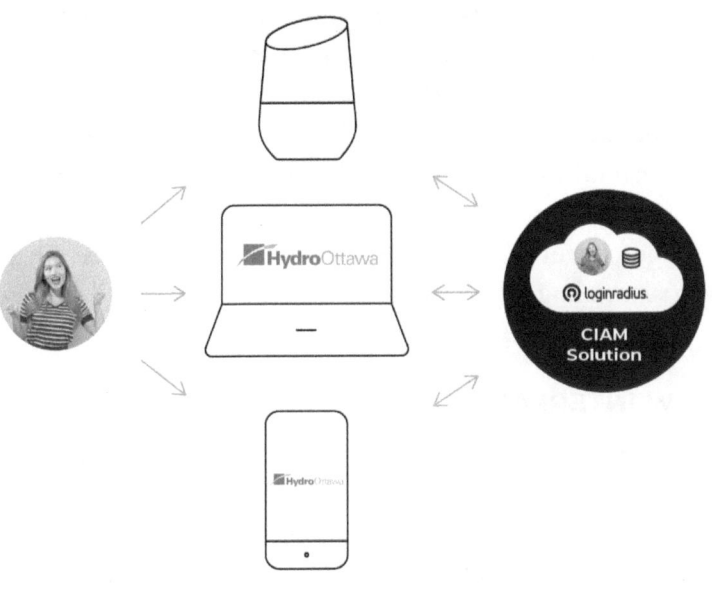

Be diligent and keep your eye on not just the new technology but also consumer behavior.

HOW TECHNOLOGY WILL EVOLVE

For decades now, login has meant entering your username and password (or email and password). But, as we know, we are rapidly entering a new age where we won't need to type anything at all. Which also means we won't need to remember things like passwords, or even write them down and store them in a safe place.

Whether desktop, laptop, tablet, or mobile phone, the device itself will recognize our voice, thumbprint, or face and let us in.

This is already a reality for some users—but not everyone.

It's still a choice. It won't be long, however, before the technologies penetrate the market to such an extent that the more traditional methods of identification and authentication dwindle and ultimately disappear.

Currently, voice and facial ID are being used only on personal devices and in one's personal zone, so to speak.

Soon it will be everywhere—at home, in your office, when you're traveling, driving in your car, and more.

NEW INTERFACES

To recap: We know that (1) we're headed toward a future where we will use these new technologies to identify and authenticate users, and (2) the main elements of these new methods will be biometric, facial, and voice. But there's more: We also know that the interfaces themselves are going to look vastly different.

As IoT continues to permeate almost every aspect of our lives, so will the new ways of logging in: We'll see these in our connected cars, in all the smart devices and speakers in our homes, and more.

> Automation is transforming everything, from our homes to our offices to the way we travel.

To be clear, it's going to happen on different timelines and among different populations. For example, we believe biometrics will be big in the public sector but will take much longer to be adopted by the general public. Consumers won't necessarily be comfortable sharing their fingerprints and biometric information with private companies, but governments already possess a lot of that information—and will leverage it in providing public services to their citizens.

In India, for example, we already see how citizen identity profiles lean heavily on biometrics, and people are using their thumbprints to access government services, pay taxes, and more. In fact, some airports in India are now using biometrics for check-ins, scanning passengers' thumbs to detect their identities, so there's no need to carry a boarding pass anymore.

Even though this trend is bound to spread to countries around the world, most likely it will stay—for now—primarily in the public sector, in government-controlled environments, with security services and such. There are simply too many privacy and security concerns (once your fingerprint is out there, obviously you can't change it or get a new one like you would an ATM card!) for biometrics to really pick up in the private sector, at least not in the next five to seven years.

It's a different story, however, with facial recognition. We believe this technology is going to pick up significantly across the board, with two big trends driving the trajectory. First, of course, facial recognition requires a camera, and cameras are everywhere, in every device. So the foundation is already there. But then you also have all the advancements happening in artificial intelligence, which are making it so much cheaper and easier for companies to use technology to identify humans more and more accurately.

For both these reasons, we believe facial recognition technologies—i.e., camera input supported by artificial intelligence—will be picking up in every industry and every vertical in the coming years.

It's going to happen quickly and will have profound effects not just on security—where only someone whose face is recognized will have authorized access to a home or office—but in so many ways we can't even imagine. In 2019, for example, facial recognition was used (this was in India again) to successfully identify thirty to forty lost kids. Typically, when a child runs away or is abandoned at an early age, identifying the child at a later age is very difficult.

AI-powered facial recognition technology makes this kind of detection possible.

> We are moving to a passwordless era where identification and authentication is powered by verification code or links, biometrics, facial ID, and voice ID.

Finally, we expect to see facial recognition become a helpful and easy-to-use second factor in two-factor authentication. Think about it like this: Currently when you use Gmail, it asks for your username and password, and then it may also send you an activation code on your phone as a second means of verification.

This two-factor approach is quite common and an important security measure. But it's admittedly clunky.

With facial recognition as secondary verification, the process becomes much smoother—the camera recognizes your face and you're in.

All in all, it's easy to see how facial recognition is poised to emerge as a preferred authentication method. We believe that voice recognition is likely to do the same. But what we've seen so far—with the consumer trend of using voice as an input and output device with Alexa, asking Google "What's the temperature?" and so on—is only the first step.

Voice authentication has not picked up yet. In the next three to eight years, however, we expect that voice authentication will see its own tipping point.

This will happen, of course, when AI is finally able to recognize distinct voices with the superior accuracy required for the technology to take off in the marketplace.

THE ROLE OF AI

At its core, AI is a machine's ability to perform cognitive tasks mostly associated with human intelligence.

For example, imagine you are at the airport, and you're stepping up to an automated kiosk for check-in. AI will quickly analyze your facial features against its biometric database and verify your identity almost instantly. This streamlined process enhances both security and elevates your check-in experience.

> Reduced wait time equals minimal stress.

Now, the question is, how does AI fit into common CIAM use cases? A good example is AI-powered adaptive multifactor authentication (Adaptive MFA)—which essentially evaluates the risk of each login attempt based on factors such as location, device type, and prior behavior. If the login occurs from a familiar device in a recognized location, AI may allow access without requiring additional authentication steps. However, if the login is attempted from an unusual device or geographic area, AI will enforce stricter security measures, such as requiring biometric verification or a second authentication factor.

AI also makes managing user roles and permissions easier. Instead of manually updating who has access to what, AI can automatically adjust access based on a user's role and behavior. This way, users get the access they need when they need it, but they also keep future sessions secure and efficient as their roles evolve.

AI is also great at identity proofing by analyzing facial recognition, document validation, or even video verification. For example, during customer onboarding, AI can verify a user's identity by comparing a live selfie with an uploaded photo ID or government document. AI algorithms analyze patterns like facial landmarks and document authenticity to quickly and securely validate the user's identity, reducing fraud while improving the user experience.

Voice authentication is another way AI is revolutionizing CIAM. Picture calling customer service. Instead of going through a lengthy verification process, AI uses voice recognition to create a personalized voiceprint based on the caller's speech patterns, tone, and accent. The next time they call, AI compares their live speech to this voiceprint in real time. If it matches, the caller is instantly verified. But if an impostor tries to gain access, AI detects the mismatch and flags the call for additional verification.

Also, there is behavioral analytics—which essentially involves how a user types, moves the mouse, or navigates a site. Imagine logging into an app, and instead of having to type in a code or answer security questions, AI analyzes their unique habits in real time. If these behaviors align with the already-established user profile, the individual is authenticated without requiring additional verification steps, like entering a one-time code.

AI doesn't stop at just logging the user in—it continuously monitors actions throughout their session, such as navigation patterns, typing speed, and device usage. If any unusual behavior is detected, such as abnormally fast clicking or irregular navigation, AI can flag the session for further review, request reauthentication, or automatically terminate the session. This all happens in real time, so threats can be handled before they even become a problem.

AI brings a touch of personalization to CIAM by integrating with chatbots and virtual assistants too. For example, when a user logs into a customer support portal, AI assesses their profile and customizes the experience based on their role and permissions. A premium customer might get access to exclusive content or services without needing to talk to a human agent. Meanwhile, other users might see more standard options tailored to their access level. This intelligent, role-based authorization not only makes interactions more efficient but also ensures that users get the right level of access with minimal effort.

Regarding consent management, AI helps platforms comply with regulations like GDPR by dynamically managing user consent. If AI notices that a user frequently interacts with certain services or content, it can predict and adjust consent options in real time, making the process smoother while keeping compliance in check.

Then again, for enterprises utilizing multiple identity providers, AI streamlines federated identity management by learning users' preferred login methods and optimizing the process accordingly.

AI is also leading the troop in passwordless authentication. Instead of remembering complex passwords, companies can rely on biometrics—like fingerprints or voice recognition—while it continuously monitors user behavior in the background.

So, there you go; by bringing AI into CIAM systems, companies can provide a smarter, more adaptable approach to managing identities and access. It's like having a security system that knows who you are, understands your routines, and adapts to changes—all while working in the background to keep things secure.

The result? A win-win situation where security and user experience are both significantly enhanced. However, AI also introduces new security risks. Bad actors are using AI to steal data and break into customer accounts with greater precision. It is important that you recognize these threats and adapt your security strategies accordingly. More on this in the section "How Security Will Evolve."

THE INTERNET OF THINGS

In other cases, of course, the technology itself is radically changing, which is what we're seeing with IoT interfaces like smart speakers, digicams, or automated cars. This trend is only going to grow, with more and more of our household appliances (doorbells, thermostats) and the items that make up our daily lives (listening to music in our car) connected to the internet.

Businesses need to look at how their consumers are interacting with and responding to these IoT interfaces, what these users are getting comfortable with, what they like, and what they don't like. For example, many of the devices already on the market use voice as an input and output, and this seems to be catching on in a big way.

Not every IoT device will be applicable to you and your business. For example, if you're a music company, you may not gain much insight from looking at how people interact with their smart thermostat. But a connected car should be of great interest to you, given that people play music in their cars.

With the newfound popularity of smart speakers, we would say that everyone should probably pay attention to them. Other IoT devices may take longer to catch on, but by 2024, smart speakers will be everywhere—and it won't be long after that before voice becomes the chosen method of authentication for these speakers.

> Our prediction is that smart speakers will become as ubiquitous in coming years as mobile phones.

In fact, what we expect to see and what we need to keep our eyes on, with all of these new interfaces, is how they interact, in remarkable ways, with the new methods of authentication: biometric, facial, and voice.

Let's say, for example, you have a lock on your door that is connected to the internet. It is a biometric lock—so now all you need to do is touch it and it will recognize your thumbprint and open automatically.

That's just one illustration of how these technologies can and will make us safer.

It is certainly an exciting time. Digital identity is being transformed before our very eyes—similar to the changes that happened when we moved from analog to digital. We welcome these exciting new tools to help deliver experience and win user trust.

But with change comes challenges.

Now that sensitive information like biometric data is being used for authentication, and becoming available to third parties, it is essential that security protocols evolve alongside the technology to protect users' identities.

HOW SECURITY WILL EVOLVE

There's no getting around the fact that as digital continues to swallow the world—with more and more services moving online and more and more data stored there—new security threats are constantly emerging and will continue to do so. In this ever-changing environment, bad actors are going to keep coming up with new ideas to break in, breach the systems, and steal information.

Sounds quite alarming, we know. But keep in mind that while all of this is happening, there are also good actors on the other side, working to combat these threats by coming up with new standards, protocols, and technologies.

Even the ways we store the data in the back end are going to change quite a bit, with the sensitive information becoming incredibly difficult to decrypt. Once this information is stored, nobody who manages the data, not even the business itself, will be able to decrypt it. There will be much more advanced security standards around storage, and more of what we call "enforced algorithms."

The point is that you, as a business, are going to have to not only keep up with changing identity technology but also, crucially, pay attention to the constant evolution happening in the security space: all the new protocols coming in and new hashing and encryption algorithms.

Like with the emerging technologies (voice recognition, etc.), you're also going to have to stay up on user behavior and how quickly and significantly the new security standards and protocols are being adopted.

When it comes to these new developments in security, we expect adoption to be very fast and widespread.

Take, for example, blockchain. In both the private and public sector, organizations are using blockchain technology to protect consumer information in a way that even if the info were to be stolen, the bad actor wouldn't be able to identify the user. In other words, they wouldn't know whose information they're breaching.

Blockchain is becoming a very important element in the digital identity space, not just in terms of storing data but also performing various identity verifications and transactions.

The evolution with blockchain is still happening, and certainly there are going to be new threats, new ways to try to breach it. But for now, what we're seeing is very impressive. What blockchain has been able to do is make it nearly impossible for any information stored to be matched with a particular user—which will protect consumers even in the event of a breach.

> Blockchain is becoming a very important element in the digital identity space.

Similarly, though AI is changing the game in CIAM, it is not always for the better. A growing threat is automated credential stuffing, where attackers use AI-powered bots to test millions of stolen username-password pairs across platforms, easily bypassing security measures (like CAPTCHA). Then there's the rise of AI-powered deepfakes—realistic videos or voice recordings that can mimic someone's face or voice, tricking even sophisticated systems or customer service reps into giving away access.

AI is also making it easier for attackers to pull off large-scale account takeovers (ATO) by exploiting weak or reused passwords, login patterns, and security questions. In addition to ATOs, AI-powered voice cloning is a growing concern, as attackers can mimic a user's voice from public samples to bypass voice-based authentication, tricking customer support or automated systems into granting access to sensitive accounts.

AI is also generating synthetic identities by blending real with fake information to create accounts that look totally legit. Today, brute-force attacks have become a lot smarter and more dangerous. Instead of randomly guessing passwords, AI can analyze common password patterns and even use compromised credentials from past breaches to target the most likely combinations in real time, drastically increasing their chances of success.

AI is learning how to bypass CAPTCHA systems, which were once a reliable defense against bots. AI systems can now mimic human behavior so well that even advanced CAPTCHA challenges can be solved. Moreover, AI is getting really good at exploiting vulnerabilities in APIs. AI tools can automatically scan for weak points in APIs and adjust attacks based on the system's response, allowing attackers to hack sensitive customer data or services.

Similar to blockchain, there are going to be many other new technologies and security practices cropping up in the next five to ten years. Unfortunately, however, very few businesses, governments, or other entities are even close to adopting these yet.

Let this be a wake-up call for you. The bad actors are not going to slow down in their efforts to infiltrate and inflict damage, for their own benefit, to you and your customers. An enduring CIAM solution must always keep pace with these malevolent moves and evolve accordingly. Businesses must change the way they currently deal with these issues and start adopting these new security technologies way faster than they are now—which is to say, they're currently not fast at all.

As the global privacy landscape undergoes rapid transformation, we can expect to witness an increased adoption of security protocols that will shape the use of digital identities by the end of the current decade.

In that same time period, we expect to see a corresponding evolution in privacy and government regulation, which we will discuss in the following section.

HOW PRIVACY WILL EVOLVE

In recent years, consumers around the world have been questioning and expressing concerns about the privacy of their personal information. Pressure is building on governments in many different countries, and legislation is already happening in a lot of places.

For example, there was the EU's GDPR law, which came into effect in 2018, allowing citizens to access their own information stored by brands, change the information as they see fit, and even delete it if they so choose.

If businesses fail to comply, the EU can impose a penalty of up to 4 percent of a business's global revenue. In fact, many companies have already paid millions of dollars in fines for breaching these European privacy laws. And the law there is still in its early stages. It will keep evolving and likely become more and more strict, as well as more complex.

We are seeing this trend around the world. In fact, around the same time, a similar bill was passed in the United States, the California Consumer Privacy Act of 2018, which gives citizens in the country's most populous state the right to access, change, and delete their information.

Nevada was the next state to follow in California's footsteps and enact its own data privacy law, Senate Bill 220—which mandates companies to provide consumers with an official number they can call (or email address to send a request) to opt out of having their data sold by that business.

Why is it so important to put control back in consumers' hands and give these rights back to them?

Well, the fact of the matter is that in today's digital world, the information stored about you can impact your life significantly, positively and negatively. You could be a victim of financial fraud and lots of other harmful actions. We see and read in the news about these privacy breaches all the time these days.

In the government sphere, there was the NSA scandal with Edward Snowden, which reached its controversial peak when it was revealed that the American intelligence agency had been tracking the information of even German Chancellor Angela Merkel (i.e., the head of state of a strong US ally).

In the wake of that event, governments around the world started thinking about how they were going to protect their own officials, as well as their citizenry.

Consumers are understandably nervous about their own privacy. It is no surprise then that people are speaking out and that pressure is building up everywhere for governments to enact privacy laws to protect their citizens' information.

We support this trend and believe that consumers should have strong privacy rights and that businesses like yours help in protecting their privacy rights.

But we also want you to become more educated and empowered in this new era of privacy and government regulation. Just like with the technology itself (e.g., biometrics)—as well as the new security protocols required to protect users and their sensitive biometric and other personal information—the evolution of privacy regulation is coming fast and furious.

Our prediction is not only that many more governments around the world are going to start imposing their own privacy laws but also that the sheer complexity of the privacy landscape is going to grow exponentially.

The new laws will have two major themes. Some will involve protecting citizens and their information—protecting people's privacy by, say, making sure their data doesn't go outside the country. In the case of the GDPR, for example, one of the law's provisions is that it can be stored only within the EU. Governments will enforce these restrictions, as the EU has done, through penalties on businesses.

But then there is also the theme of privacy legislation, which involves giving consumers rights over their own information. We see this in both the California bill and GDPR.

> Privacy law and government regulation is about to explode around the world—what are you doing to educate and empower yourself and your business for this new era?

PUTTING IT ALL TOGETHER TO PREPARE FOR THE FUTURE

Over the course of this book, you've come to see the wisdom in embracing and executing your CIAM solution now, rather than waiting for circumstances to force you.

The good news is that, having made the decision to address your problems around identity with a single unified software solution, you and your business are so much more protected against the unknown—prepared and equipped to stay on top of future developments in technology, security, and privacy.

Of course, no one knows for sure what the future holds, which is why it's essential that your CIAM solution evolve rather than stay static. Obviously, a third-party solution makes this much easier. If you are doing it in-house, you need to constantly invest in R & D and innovation so that you are up to speed.

Even if you decide to go with a vendor, however, you're still going to need to make sure that the third party you pick has the track record of innovation so that your business is not affected. The consequences of such decisions are profound, and you must approach these matters as the mission-critical endeavors that they are, as we'll see in this next and final chapter.

CHAPTER TWENTY-ONE

KEEPING UP WITH INNOVATION

Walmart, of course, is a US business juggernaut. It is a company that everyone knows and, for better or worse, has dominated the brick-and-mortar retail market for decades. But until the mid-2010s, it hadn't kept up with new technology. It was late to the game to understand the ways consumer behavior had changed and was going digital; it didn't transition well to mobile; and now it is in an all-out war with Amazon over e-commerce market share.

The same thing—or rather, worse—has of course happened to Sears and many, many other once-successful businesses.

The same thing could easily happen to you, to put it bluntly, if you don't keep up with where we're headed in the digital identity space.

> If you're not keeping up with where we're headed in digital identity, you may very well become the new cautionary tale to others, the Blockbuster or RadioShack of your industry—don't let that happen! Make these changes now!

Everyone says they get this. They know how important innovation is. But they don't act on it. We see the same pattern all the time.

Learn from the mistakes of your competitors. Just because you have a login and authentication system that works well for you today, it certainly doesn't mean you're going to be okay for the next three or five years.

You need to continue innovating on how you interact with your consumers, how you authenticate and verify them, how you make things simpler and more streamlined, and how you develop and improve the user experience.

As we saw in the previous chapter, you have to keep up with innovations on the security and privacy side as well—this is all part of winning customers and gaining and retaining user trust.

It is essential to the survival of your CIAM strategy, and failure in these areas can critically damage your branding and your business as a whole.

But on the flip side, by outsourcing these needs to a provider whose core business and expertise is in exactly this kind of ongoing identity management—a third party who can do the R & D and keep up with the innovation themselves—the sky is the limit.

Get ahead of the game and leverage the power of digital identity now to win trust and transform user experience.

CONCLUSION

What Now?

Over the course of this book, we've taught you the ins and outs of using CIAM to deliver a secure and extraordinary experience. We've gone over the why, the what, and the how: why it matters, what it is (and what its benefits are), and how to strategize your own CIAM solution.

Now, it's up to you.

Maybe you picked up this book because you were curious but still unsure. You recognized the problems you were facing around identity and wanted to do better.

Having now come to the end of the book, how has your perspective changed?

Hopefully, you see that CIAM is not just a trend, and not some small boutique approach that only a handful of companies are experimenting with.

On the contrary, and as you have seen throughout this book, this revolution in digital identity management is poised to transform the business landscape and create new winners and losers.

What side of that equation do you want to be on? If you're determined to win, go out now, today, and begin treating this like the intense, mission-critical project that it is!

ACKNOWLEDGMENTS

I'd like to thank you for picking up my book.

For a decade, I've been working "behind the scenes," building a globally recognized, leading Customer Identity and Access Management (CIAM) platform that has revolutionized the way enterprises deliver secure and privacy-compliant customer experiences. It's been a wild ride, but I wouldn't trade it for the world.

So, I felt it was time to share my experiences through this book.

As the saying goes, "It takes a village to raise a child." Writing this book has been a huge undertaking too. It took three years' worth of research and hard work and a team of dedicated, loving, and extremely talented people to make this book happen. They were at the right place at the right time. They helped me along the way without even realizing their influence, so I want to give them a shout out.

To our incredible team at LoginRadius, thank you for being part of the family—for working with me to help hundreds of enterprise clients and over a billion consumers. You helped me gain so much knowledge over the years.

Also, special thanks to my team members who provided their valuable feedback on the manuscript and graphics. I couldn't have finished this book without you—Ajoy Anand, Karl Wittig, Kundan Singh, Ravi Teja, Vikas Jayeram, Max Sergeyenko and Navanita Devi.

I owe a huge debt of gratitude to our customers for trusting us and giving us opportunities to work with them on their CIAM projects. They allowed us to do what we do best—secure the identities of end-users and manage access—and grow into the company we are today. I especially thank ITV, City of Surrey, and Hyrdo Ottawa for letting us cover them in this book as case studies.

Special thanks to Donnie McLohon, Ellie Cole, and Sophie May, the ever-patient publishing managers.

I cannot express the appropriate amount of appreciation to my incredible editor, Mark Chait, who was ever ready to discuss nuances of my texts and pushed me to clarify concepts. Thank you for your detailed and constructive comments and for working so hard on this book.

Most importantly, I'd like to thank my family. They are the pillars of constant inspiration in my life. Their support has sustained me through many sleepless nights and weekends spent locked in front of the computer screen. Thank you all for always being there.

ABOUT THE AUTHOR

With a passion for business and creativity, Rakesh Soni has been instrumental in growing LoginRadius from a startup to a leading provider of Customer Identity and Access Management (CIAM) solutions that serves over one billion users.

Rakesh led the company's effort to bring together world-class VC firms, including Microsoft's M12, and raise $20 million in funding.

Apart from being a tech entrepreneur, Rakesh advises and invests in startups. He founded an angel group, ISM Angels, that invests $3 million per year in early-stage startups.

He is an avid reader and a writer. He regularly contributes to leading tech magazines like VentureBeat, Wired, Entrepreneur, InformationWeek, Forbes, Business.com, and more. More so, he loves to share book reviews with the world.

Rakesh has an engineering degree from the Indian Institute of Technology (IIT) and an MS from the University of Alberta.

www.ingramcontent.com/pod-product-compliance
Lightning Source LLC
LaVergne TN
LVHW041957060526
838200LV00018B/374/J